Our "Compacted" Compact Clinicals Team

Dear Valued Customer,

Welcome to Compact Clinicals. We are committed to bringing mental health professionals up-to-date, diagnostic and treatment information in a compact, timesaving, easy-to-read format. Our line of books provides current, thorough reviews of assessment and treatment strategies for mental disorders.

We've "compacted" complete information for diagnosing each disorder and comparing how different theoretical orientations approach treatment. Our books use nonacademic language, real-world examples, and well-defined terminology.

Enjoy this and other timesaving books from Compact Clinicals.

Sincerely,

Melanie A. Dean

Melanie Dean, Ph.D.
President

Compact Clinicals Line of Books

Compact Clinicals currently offers these condensed reviews for professionals:

- **Attention Deficit Hyperactivity Disorder (in Adults and Children):** *The Latest Assessment and Treatment Strategies*

- **Borderline Personality Disorder:** *The Latest Assessment and Treatment Strategies*

- **Conduct Disorders:** *The Latest Assessment and Treatment Strategies*

- **Eating Disorders:** *The Latest Assessment and Treatment Strategies*

- **Major Depressive Disorder:** *The Latest Assessment and Treatment Strategies*

- **Obsessive-Compulsive Disorder:** *The Latest Assessment and Treatment Strategies*

- **Post-Traumatic Stress Disorder:** *The Latest Assessment and Treatment Strategies*

Call for Writers

Compact Clinicals is always interested in publishing new titles in order to keep our selection of books current and comprehensive. If you have a book proposal or an idea you would like to discuss, please call or write to:

Melanie Dean, Ph.D., President
Compact Clinicals
7205 NW Waukomis Dr., Suite A
Kansas City, MO 64151
(816) 587-0044

Post-Traumatic Stress Disorder

The Latest Assessment and Treatment Strategies

by

Matthew J. Friedman, M.D., Ph.D.

Compact Clinicals...condensed reviews for professionals

Post-Traumatic Stress Disorder
The Latest Assessment and Treatment Strategies

by
Matthew J. Friedman, M.D., Ph.D.

Published by: Compact Clinicals
7205 NW Waukomis Dr., Suite A
Kansas City, MO 64151
816-587-0044

Compact Clinicals ...*condensed reviews for professionals*

Copy Editing by:
In Credible English
1800 South West Temple, Suite 501
Salt Lake City, UT 84115
Desktop Publishing by:
Cactus Tracks
1958 Five Iron Drive
Castle Rock, CO 80104
Cover Design by:
Patrick G. Handley

Library of Congress Cataloging in Publication Data

Friedman, Matthew J.
    Post traumatic stress disorder: the latest assessment and treatment strategies / by
    Matthew J. Friedman
        p. cm.
    Includes bibliographical references and index.
    ISBN 1-887537-14-7 (pbk.)
      1. Post-traumatic stress disorder. I. Title.

    RC552.P67 F75 2000
    616.85'21–dc21
    for Library of Congress   00-021872
                                                                      CIP

ISBN 1-887537-14-7

Read Me First

As a mental health professional, often the information you need can only be obtained after countless hours of reading or library research. If your schedule precludes this time commitment, Compact Clinicals is the answer.

Our books are practitioner oriented with easy-to-read treatment descriptions and examples. Compact Clinicals books are written in a nonacademic style. Our books are formatted to make the first reading as well as ongoing reference quick and easy. You will find:

- **Anecdotes** — Each chapter begins and ends with a fictionalized account that personalizes the disorder. These accounts include a **"Dear Diary"** entry at the beginning of each chapter that illustrates a typical client's viewpoint about their disorder. Each chapter ends with **"File Notes"** of a fictional therapist, Pat Owen. These **"File Notes"** address assessment, diagnosis, and treatment considerations for the "client" writing the **"Dear Diary"** entries.

- **Sidebars** — Narrow columns on the outside of each page highlight important information, preview upcoming sections or concepts, and define terms used in the text.

- **Definitions** — Terms are defined in the sidebars where they originally appear in the text and in an alphabetical glossary on pages 91 through 94.

- **References** — Numbered references appear in the text following information from that source. Full references appear in a bibliography on pages 95 through 104.

- **Case Examples** — Our examples illustrate typical client comments or conversational exchanges that help clarify different treatment approaches. Identifying information in the examples (e.g., the individual's real name, profession, age, and/or location) has been changed to protect the confidentiality of those clients discussed in case examples.

Acknowledgement

The author wishes to thank Elaine Baldwin, Lucy Berliner, John Fairbank, Terence Keane, Patricia Resick, Susan Solomon, Farris Tuma and John Wilson who carefully reviewed an earlier draft of this book and suggested many important revisions.

Contents

Chapter One: Overview of Post-Traumatic Stress Disorder (PTSD) 1
What is Trauma? 1
What are PTSD and ASD, and How are They Different? 3
How Common Is PTSD? 4
What is the Likelihood of Recovery? 4

Chapter Two: Diagnosing and Assessing PTSD 7
What are Typical Characteristics of Those with PTSD? 7
Figure 2.1 — Typical Characteristics of Those with PTSD 8
What Criteria Are Used to Diagnose PTSD? 10
The Traumatic Stress Criterion 10
Figure 2.2 — The Exposure A$_1$ Criterion 10
Figure 2.3 — DSM-IV Diagnostic Criteria for PTSD 12
Example: Traumatic Event — Criterion A 13
Example: Reexperciencing Symptoms — Criterion B 14
Example: Avoidant/Numbing Symptoms — Criterion C 15
Example: Hyperarousal Symptoms — Criterion D 16
Similiarities and Differences Between PTSD & ASD 17
What Tools are Available for Clinical Assessment? 18
The Clinical Interview 19
General Considerations 19
Risk Factors 20
Self-report Instruments and Structured Interviews 20
Figure 2.4 — Risk Factors for PTSD 21
Psychometric Instruments 22
What Differentiates PTSD from Other Disorders? 22
Figure 2.5 — PTSD Assessment Scales 23
Comorbid Disorders 23
Figure 2.6 — DSM-IV Disorders Frequently Comorbid with PTSD 25
Medical Disorders 25
Other "Unofficial" Post-Traumatic Syndromes 25

Chapter Three: Psychological Treatments for PTSD 27
What are the Global Treatment Issues Related to PTSD? 27
Why is Help Sought Now? 28
Is Treating PTSD the First Order of Business? 29
Psychiatric Emergency 29
Alcohol or Drug Abuse/Dependence 29
Co-Existing Psychiatric Disorders 30
Situational Factors 30
What General Issues Must be Considered When Choosing
a Specific Treatment Option? 31
Combined Treatment 32
Treatment of Comorbid Disorders 32
"Complex PTSD" 32

Cross-Cultural Considerations 33
Recovered Memories 33
What are the Major Personal Issues for Clinicians When Treating
    Someone with PTSD? 34
Therapeutic Neutrality vs. Advocacy 35
Vicarious Traumatization 35
Countertransference 36
Clinician Self-Care... 36
What Psychological Treatments are Available for Adults with PTSD? 37
General Stages and Focus of Treatment 37
Establishing Trust and Safety 38
Trauma Focus vs. Supportive Therapy.. 38
Integration 39
Global Therapies 39
Psychological Debriefing 39
Psychoeducation 42
Peer Counseling 43
Individual Psychotherapies 44
Cognitive Behavioral Therapy (CBT) 44
Exposure Therapy 46
Cognitive Therapy 47
Cognitive Processing Therapy (CPT) 48
Biofeedback and Relaxation Training 49
Systematic Desensitization (SD) 49
Assertiveness Training 50
Stress Inoculation Training (SIT) 51
Psychodynamic Psychotherapy... 53
Eye Movement Desensitization and Reprocessing (EMDR) 54
Marital/Family Therapies 56
Group Therapies 57
Psychodynamic Focus Group Therapy 58
Cognitive Behavioral Focus Group Therapy 58
Supportive Group Therapy 58
Social Rehabilitative Therapies 59
What Psychological Treatments are Available for Children
and Adolescents with PTSD, and How Effective Are Those Treatments? 61
Cognitive Behavioral Therapy 61
Psychological Debriefing 62
Art and Play Therapy 62
Stress Inoculation Training (SIT) 62
Psychoeducational Approaches for Parents, Teachers and Children 63

Chapter 4: Medical Treatments for PTSD **65**
How Does the Human Stress Response Relate to PTSD? **65**
Fight or Flight Reaction 66
The General Adaptation Syndrome 66
Figure 4.1 — Human Stress Response 67

What Psychobiological Abnormalities
Exist for Those With PTSD? **68**
    Alterations in Brain Structure 68
    Adrenergic System 68
    HPA System 69
    Serotonergic System 69
    Corticotropin Releasing Factor (CRF) 69
    Neurotransmission 70
What Medical Treatments Are Used for PTSD? **71**
    Selective Serotonin Reuptake Inhibitors (SSRIs) 71
    Figure 4.2 — Evidence for Efficacy of Medications in the Treatment of PTSD 72
    Other Serotonergic Antidepressants 74
    Monoamine Oxidase Inhibitors (MAOIs) 74
    Tricyclic Antidepressants (TCAs) 74
    Anti-adrenergic Agents: Propranolol and Clonidine 75
    Antianxiety Agents 76
    Anticonvulsants 76
    Antipsychotics 76
    What is a Good Strategy for PTSD Pharmacotherapy? 77

Appendix A: PTSD Assessment Tools for Adults **79**
Trauma Exposure Scales **79**
    General Traumatic Experiences 79
    Specific Traumatic Experiences 80
        Childhood Trauma 80
        Domestic Violence 81
        War-zone Trauma 82
        Torture 82
Diagnostic Instruments **82**
PTSD Symptom Severity Scales **84**
Symptom Severity Scales for Acute Stress Disorder (ASD) **86**

Appendix B: PTSD Assessment Tools for Children **87**
Trauma Exposure Scales **87**
Diagnostic Instruments **89**
PTSD Symptom Severity Scales **89**

Glossary **91**
Bibliography **95**
Index **105**

You will be following a typical client's thoughts about their disorder through the "Dear Diary" notes at the beginning of each chapter. At the end of each chapter, a fictional therapist's "File Notes" will reflect the assessment and treatment of the client writing the "Dear Diary" notes.

Chapter One: Overview of Post-Traumatic Stress Disorder (PTSD)

> *Diary of Mary T.*
>
> March 5
>
> That lawyer called again. He thinks I've got a great case against the trucking company and could win a huge settlement. It's tempting. I certainly need the money. But every time I even think about the accident (like now) I go to pieces. And—if I start to talk about it, I get terrified. Then the nightmares. No sleep. That horrible jumpy feeling. And I turn into a nervous wreck. It isn't worth it, even if I could win a million bucks!!! I'll just have to call him back tomorrow and tell him I'm not interested. He'll have to find someone else to sue.

This chapter answers the following:

- **What is Trauma?** — This section defines trauma, the necessary precursor to PTSD.

- **What are PTSD and ASD, and How are They Different?** — This section defines, compares, and contrasts PTSD and ASD.

- **How Common Is PTSD?** — This section examines prevalence for this disorder.

- **What is the Likelihood of Recovery?** — This section discusses expected outcomes for those with PTSD.

During the course of a lifetime, approximately half of all men and women will be exposed to at least one traumatic event, such as assault, military combat, an industrial or vehicular accident, rape, domestic violence, or a natural disaster (e.g., an earthquake). Although most people can absorb the psychological impact of such an experience and resume their normal lives, a sizable minority (approximately 8 percent) will suffer significant distress or impairment in social, occupational or other important areas of functioning.[1]

What is Trauma?

"Trauma" was first introduced in the *DSM-III* as a catastrophic stressor that "would evoke significant symptoms of distress in most people."[2] Trauma was characterized as a rare and overwhelming event that differed qualitatively from "common experiences such as bereavement, chronic illness, business losses or marital conflict." Traumatic events cited in

DSM-III — *Diagnostic and Statistical Manual of Mental Disorders - Third Edition.* This manual, published by the American Psychiatric Association, is the authoritative source on psychiatric diagnosis

For specific PTSD diagnostic criteria, see pages 12-13.

DSM-III included: rape, assault, torture, incarceration in a death camp, military combat, natural disasters, industrial/vehicular accidents, torture, or exposure to war/civil/domestic violence. Although the list of potential traumatic events has changed little since 1980, our understanding about trauma has changed significantly, particularly in relation to the prevalence and psychological impacts of catastrophic events. Specifically:

- **Catastrophic events are not rare.** Research in the United States indicates that over half of all American men (60.7 percent) and women (51.2 percent) will likely be exposed to at least one catastrophic event during their lives.[1] Exposure prevalence is obviously much higher in countries torn by war, civil strife, genocide, state-sponsored terrorism, or other forms of violence.

- **Trauma is not just an external event.** The concept of trauma has changed from a rare, external event (as defined in DSM-III) to an individual's psychological response to an overwhelming event (as defined in *DSM-IV*).

DSM-IV — <u>Diagnostic and Statistical Manual of Mental Disorders - Fourth Edition</u>

Initially researchers thought that trauma could be defined exclusively in terms of catastrophic events that happened to individuals who were in the wrong place at the wrong time. As initially conceptualized, anyone exposed to war, rape, torture, or natural disaster, would be "traumatized."[2] This approach changed in the 1994 DSM-IV because most people exposed to catastrophic events failed to develop PTSD.[3] For example, research indicates 54 percent of American women who have been raped do not develop PTSD; 91 percent of American women involved in an accident do not develop PTSD.[1] Although exposure to catastrophic stress is a necessary condition, it is insufficient by itself to "traumatize" an individual. The critical discriminator is the person's emotional response to such an event. If the rape or accident produces an intense emotional response (characterized in the DSM-IV as "fear, helplessness, or horror") the event is "traumatic." If an event does not produce an intense emotional response, then the event is not considered a "traumatic event" and, according to the DSM definition, cannot cause PTSD.

Poets and writers for many years have recognized that exposure to trauma may produce enduring psychological consequences, including Homer's <u>Iliad</u>[4] and Shakespeare's <u>Henry IV</u>. Clinicians' attention, in the late 19th century, began to focus on the psychological as well as the physiological impact of military combat among U.S. Civil War and European Franco-Prussian War veterans. Physiological symptoms were interpreted as cardiovascular syndromes (e.g., Soldier's Heart, Da Costa' Syndrome, Neurocirculatory Asthenia) while psychiatric symptoms produced diagnoses of Nostalgia, Shell Shock, Combat Fatigue, War Neurosis.[5] Throughout this period, clinicians who were asked to provide treatment for survivors of military or civilian trauma were struck by the physiological as well as psychological symptoms exhibited.[6-8]

Clinical presentations among 19th century civilian survivors of train accidents were called Railway Spine.[6]

Although recognized by other names since antiquity and by modern psychiatry since the late 1800s, PTSD was first defined as a distinct psychiatric diagnosis in 1980 when the American Psychiatric Association published the DSM-III.[2] Further, until the Diagnostic and Statistical Manual of Mental Disorders - Fourth Edition (DSM-IV), there was no diagnosis that could be given to an individual who may have suffered great distress during the immediate aftermath of a traumatic event, but who recovered within a month's time. For example, prior to inclusion of Acute Stress Disorder (ASD) in the DSM-IV, military psychiatrists named such acute reactions as "combat stress reaction" or "battle fatigue."

A very good description of the ASD phenomenon can be found in Stephen Crane's novel about the Civil War, The Red Badge of Courage, in which the protagonist, a new recruit to the Union Army, has a classic ASD attack during his first exposure to enemy gunfire.

What are PTSD and ASD, and How are they Different?

When people experience a traumatic stressor, they may experience severe and incapacitating psychological distress. Symptoms can include nightmares, avoidance of people, places, and other stimuli associated with the trauma. When these symptoms occur as part of the normal, immediate human response to overwhelming events but subside within a month, clinicians can diagnose Acute Stress Disorder (ASD). If, however, the symptoms persist beyond one month, the client may meet the criteria for Post-Traumatic Stress Disorder (PTSD).

ASD symptoms for the most part are similar to those for PTSD; however, an individual need only exhibit one each reexperiencing, avoidant, and hyperarousal symptoms to be diagnosed with ASD. Individuals must exhibit more symptoms from these clusters over a longer period of time to be diagnosed with PTSD.

See pages 12 and 13 for diagnostic criteria of PTSD.

The major difference between ASD and PTSD is the greater emphasis placed on symptoms of *dissociation* in ASD. With dissociation, normal mental functions such as memory, sense of time, or sense of one's body or personal identity as a coherent entity, may be severely distorted. Dissociative symptoms

dissociation — an abnormal psychological state in which one's perception of oneself and/ or one's environment is altered significantly must be present in ASD, but not in PTSD. Acutely traumatized individuals need exhibit only one symptom from the reexperiencing, avoidance, and hyperarousal clusters; however, meeting ASD diagnostic criteria requires exhibiting three dissociative symptoms.

Everyone who exhibits ASD does not develop PTSD. Furthermore, people who never exhibit ASD sometimes develop PTSD later on. There is very little research to guide us on the relationship between these two disorders; however, it appears that most people with ASD are at a much greater risk to develop PTSD than those who do not develop PTSD.[9-12]

How Common Is PTSD?

Today, PTSD is considered a significant public health problem that can affect millions of Americans. Eight percent of Americans (5 percent of men and 10 percent of women) will develop PTSD at some point in their lives.[1] If untreated, many individuals will never recover. For example, research with World War II veterans and Nazi Holocaust survivors shows that PTSD can persist for over 50 years or for a lifetime.[13]

What is the Likelihood of Recovery?

PTSD is no different than other medical or psychiatric disorders in that its severity may vary from mild to severe. As with diabetes, heart disease, and depression, some people with PTSD are able to lead full and rewarding lives despite the disorder. However, a minority may develop a persistent, incapacitating mental illness marked by severe and intolerable symptoms; marital, social and vocational disability; and extensive use of psychiatric and community services.[14] The long-term course for most people with chronic PTSD is marked by remissions and relapses. Some make a full recovery, others experience partial improvement, others never improve. Three general classes exist for those with PTSD:

Education for family and friends of those with PTSD promotes requests by PTSD sufferers for treatment and thereby facilitates recovery.

1. **Lifetime PTSD** – Forty percent of those who develop PTSD will likely not recover whether or not they have ever received treatment. Some may show improvement in functional capacity or symptom severity, but their PTSD remains chronic, severe, and permanent.[1]

2. **PTSD in Remission with Occasional Relapses** – Clients in remission who experience sudden relapses and begin to exhibit the full pattern of PTSD symptoms have probably been recently exposed to a situation that resembled the original traumatic event in a significant way. For example, many Japanese survivors of the World War II bombing of Kobe (who had functioned well for decades) had a relapse of PTSD symptoms following the 1995 major earthquake there. They reported that the physical sensations (rumbling and tremors of the earthquake), the enormous death and destruction that surrounded them, and the threat to life of loved ones and themselves, evoked long dormant memories and feelings resulting from the bombing attacks 50 years ago.

3. **Delayed Onset** – There is a delayed variant of PTSD in which individuals exposed to a traumatic event do not exhibit the PTSD syndrome until months or years afterwards. As with relapse, the immediate precipitant is usually a situation that resembles the original trauma in a significant way. For example, an American Vietnam veteran whose child has been suddenly deployed to participate in a dangerous United Nations peacekeeping operation may experience PTSD symptoms.

Chapter 2 reviews specific diagnostic criteria for PTSD as well as assessment strategies and instruments. Chapter 3 reviews psychological treatments for PTSD while chapter 4 reviews biological treatments for PTSD.

**Therapy Notes
from the Desk
of Pat Owen**

April 18

*Client is a twenty-seven-year-old woman who lost her husband
last year when a large truck ran through a red light, smashing
into the car she was driving, killing her husband and trapping her
inside. She reports extreme distress during the episode: fear,
grief, rage. She reports recurrent nightmares and daytime
thoughts about the accident. She tries to avoid seeing and
hearing trucks, refuses to drive a car, and feels numb inside. Also
reports insomnia, irritability, and feeling jumpy and "watchful" all
the time. She also feels depressed and guilty; won't eat; doesn't
want to see anyone.*

*No previous personal or family psychiatric history. Probably
PTSD. May also have Major Depressive Disorder.*

Chapter Two: Diagnosing and Assessing PTSD

Diary of Mary T

May 20

Well, I did it!! I sat through two hours with that doctor. I couldn't believe there were so many questions. I also couldn't believe that so many of them seemed to fit. Right on target about all that's been bothering me. I did pretty well at first. And I didn't mind telling her what a mess I've been. How my nerves are shot. The nightmares. And all the rest. But when she started asking about the accident, I lost it. I just couldn't go on. And I'm getting so upset just thinking about it that I'd better stop right now.

This chapter answers the following:

• **What are Typical Characteristics of Those with PTSD?** — This section focuses on the key symptoms of PTSD: reexperiencing, avoidant/numbing, and hyperarousal.

• **What Criteria are Used to Diagnose PTSD?** — This section presents information on the DSM-IV criteria for PTSD with a case history that illustrates each symptom. The main differences between PTSD and ASD are reviewed.

• **What Tools are Available for Clinical Assessment?** — This section addresses clinical issues pertinent to conducting a successful diagnostic interview, diagnostic instruments currently available for both disorders, and reviews research data on risk factors for PTSD.

• **What Differentiates PTSD from Other Disorders?** — This section reviews other disorders that commonly co-exist with PTSD.

What are Typical Characteristics of Those with PTSD?

PTSD is characterized by the requirement that a person must have been traumatized by a catastrophic stressor and consists of three symptom clusters (reexperiencing, avoidant/numbing, and hyperarousal as shown in Figure 2.1) as well as diagnostic criteria for persistence and severity.

Reexperiencing Symptoms — These symptoms are unique to PTSD in relation to other psychiatric disorders. They reflect the persistence of thoughts, feelings, and behaviors specifically related to the traumatic event. Such recollections are intrusive because they are not only unwanted, but are also powerful enough to drive away consideration of anything else. Daytime recollections and traumatic nightmares often evoke panic, terror, dread, grief, or despair among those with PTSD. Sometimes people with PTSD are exposed to reminders of the

Figure 2.1 — Typical Characteristics of Those with PTSD		
Reexperiencing Symptoms	**Avoidant/Numbing Symptoms**	**Hyperarousal Symptoms**
• Intrusive recollections • Traumatic nightmares • PTSD flashbacks • Trauma-related, stimulus-evoked psychological distress • Trauma-related, stimulus-evoked physiological reactions	• Efforts to avoid trauma-related thoughts and feelings • Efforts to avoid trauma-related activities, places, and people • *Psychogenic amnesia* for trauma-related memories • Diminished interest • Feeling detached or being estranged • Restricted range of affect • Sense of foreshortened future	• Insomnia • Irritability • Difficulty concentrating • Hypervigilance • Exaggerated startle response

*psychogenic amnesia —
the inability to remember
emotionally charged events
for psychological rather
than neurological reasons*

*Reexperiencing can elicit
symptoms of psychological
distress (e.g., terror) or
abnormal physiological
reactions (e.g., a racing
pulse, rapid breathing,
or sweating).*

trauma (trauma-related stimuli), and are suddenly thrust into an intense psychological, emotional, and/or physiological state. Trauma-related stimuli can precipitate PTSD flashbacks, in which clients actually relive the traumatic experience, losing all connection with the present. In these acute dissociative or brief psychotic states, they actually behave as if they must protect themselves or fight for their lives as was the case during the initial trauma.

Example

A woman was raped at dusk by an assailant who sprang out of the shadows opening onto an urban thoroughfare. He dragged her into the recesses of a dark alley before beginning his sexual assault. It is now many months later. She is walking home from work. The setting sun produces shadows over every nook and cranny adjacent to the sidewalk. As she glances into a heavily shadowed alley, she actually "sees" an assailant poised and ready to grab her. In fact, no one is there. The similarity between the visual stimuli present during the rape scene several months ago and those produced today by an urban sunset have produced an *hallucination* or PTSD flash-

*hallucination — sensory
perceptions without
external stimulation;
hearing voices or seeing
things others do not*

> back. As a result, the woman believes that she is, again, about to be raped and runs down the street, screaming in terror.

Avoidant/Numbing Symptoms — These symptoms are behavioral, cognitive, or emotional strategies used to ward off the terror and distress caused by reexperiencing symptoms, including:

- **Avoidant Symptoms:** Avoiding thoughts, feelings, activities, places, and people related to the original traumatic event or psychogenic amnesia for trauma-related memories.

> **Example**
>
> A 10-year-old refugee who witnessed the massacre of his father and brothers and the rape of his mother by paramilitary troops cannot remember this horrible episode. He remembers that the soldiers came to the house, that he ran, hid, and eventually escaped. But he cannot remember what happened in between.

- **Numbing symptoms:** These are psychological mechanisms through which PTSD sufferers anesthetize themselves against the intolerable panic, terror, and pain evoked by reexperiencing symptoms. *Psychic numbing* occurs when PTSD sufferers automatically suppress most feelings to block out intolerable ones. This strategy comes at a very high price however, because in order to numb intolerable trauma-related feelings, one must also anesthetize the loving feelings that are necessary to sustain any intimate, loving relationship.

Hyperarousal Symptoms — These symptoms are the most apparent manifestations of PTSD's excessive physiologic arousal and include insomnia, irritability, startle reactions, and hypervigilance. Such a *hyper-reactive psychophysiological state* makes it very difficult for people with PTSD to concentrate or perform other cognitive tasks. This cluster of PTSD symptoms most closely resembles symptoms seen in *Panic Disorder* and *Generalized Anxiety Disorder* and is one reason why PTSD has been classified in the DSM-IV as an Anxiety Disorder.

psychic numbing — is the inability to feel any emotions, either positive, such as love and pleasure, or negative, such as fear or guilt, also described as an "emotional anesthesia"

hyper-reactive psychophysiological state — a state in which emotions are heightened and aroused and even minor events may produce a state in which the heart pounds rapidly, muscles tense, and there is great overall agitation

Panic Disorder — a psychiatric disorder marked by intense anxiety and panic including symptoms such as palpitations, shortness of breath, and sweating

Generalized Anxiety Disorder — a psychiatric disorder marked by unrealistic worry, apprehension, and uncertainty

For information on distinguishing Panic Disorder and Generalized Anxiety Disorder from PTSD, see pages 22-25.

What Criteria are Used to Diagnose PTSD?

This section presents diagnostic criteria and examples of
PTSD symptoms. It also reviews similarities and differences
between the symptoms of PTSD and Acute Stress Disorder,
(ASD). Common to both disorders is the definition of a traumatic event, which consists of two components:[3]

1. Exposure to a catastrophic event (the A_1 criterion)

2. Emotional distress due to such exposure (the A_2 criterion)

The Traumatic Stress Criterion

Figure 2.2 shows the DSM-IV definition of the A_1 criterion
and illustrative examples.

Figure 2.2 — The Exposure A_1 Criterion

"Exposure" Encompasses...	Examples Include...
Catastrophic events that involve actual or threat-ened death or serious injury (those directly involved or those who witness the event).	Military combat Interpersonal violence (e.g., sexual assault, physical attack, torture) Manmade/natural disasters Accidents Incarceration Exposure to war zone/urban/domestic violence
Those who witness the aftermath of a catastrophic event, but were never in personal danger.	Witnessing body parts or devastation resulting from the catastrophic event
Those who are "confronted with" the results/facts of a life-threatening event.	Learning that a loved one has died or been seriously injured

Example

"Mothers of the Disappeared" is a term used for
women whose children were arrested by police
during state-sponsored terrorism (military dicta-
torship). During this "Dirty War," the military
junta arrested, incarcerated, tortured, and often
executed individuals whom they considered sub-
versive. The mothers often witnessed the arrest of
their children, but they witnessed nothing more.

In all cases, however, the continued disappearance of their children meant they probably had been executed. According to DSM-IV, these mothers have all suffered exposure to an A_1 event, because they have been "confronted with" the probable execution of their children.

People are different. Some people exposed to an A_1 event will experience severe psychological distress (meeting the A_2 criterion for PTSD, characterized in the DSM-IV as "fear, helplessness, or horror"; others will not experience significant distress (not warranting a PTSD diagnosis); and still others may have a delayed response (leading to PTSD).

Example

Young children who have been sexually abused may not have experienced significant distress (an A_2 response) at the time of the sexual assault. Years later (often as adolescents or adults), long after the abuse has stopped, they may realize that they were coerced to participate in such sexual behavior by a powerful adult against whom they were helpless and on whom they were dependent. Such retrospective reconstruction may transform a complicated and vaguely uncomfortable memory into a shocking recollection of an A_1 sexual assault. The new emotional response to what has just become re-conceptualized as an A_1 event may now be experienced as fear, helplessness, or horror. The person has thus transformed a childhood memory into an abusive traumatic experience, and may possibly develop PTSD.

A_1 events differ considerably in their capacity to evoke psychological distress. For example, suffering injury because of a perpetrator's willful, violent, personal intent is much more distressing than suffering injury because of an impersonal accident or natural disaster. This is a major reason why 46 percent of women who have been raped develop PTSD in comparison to only 9 percent of women involved in an accident.[1]

Some people are exposed to catastrophic A_1 events continually because of their professional responsibilities (e.g., military, police, emergency medical personnel, and mental health professionals). As a result, they may be at greater risk to experience A_2 distress. However, it is by no means certain that they will do so. Furthermore, effective measures can help professionals cope with an A_1 response when it does occur. (See chapter 3.)

Children (especially those six and younger) who lack an adult's capacity for abstract thinking or linguistic expression may express their emotional reaction (A_2 reaction) behaviorally rather than verbally or regress to an earlier developmental stage. They typically do this through non-verbal indicators of psychological distress (e.g., disorganized or agitated behavior or indicators that appear during play).

Figure 2.3 —DSM-IV Diagnostic Criteria for Post-Traumatic Stress Disorder

(The following has been reprinted with permission by the American Psychiatric Association: Diagnostic and Statistical Manual of Mental Disorder, Fourth Edition. Washington DC: American Psychiatric Association, 1994)

A. The person has been exposed to a traumatic event in which both of the following were present:

1. the person experienced, witnessed, or was confronted with an event or events that involved actual or threatened death or serious injury, or a threat to the physical integrity of self or others

2. the person's response involved intense fear, helplessness, or horror

B. The traumatic event is persistently reexperienced in one (or more) of the following ways:

1. recurrent and intrusive distressing recollections of the event, including images, thoughts, or perceptions

2. recurrent distressing dreams of the event

3. acting or feeling as if the traumatic event were recurring (includes a sense of reliving the experience, illusions, hallucinations, and dissociative *flashback episodes*

4&5. intense psychological distress or *physiological reactivity* at exposure to internal or external clues that symbolize or resemble an aspect of the traumatic event

C. Persistent avoidance of stimuli associated with the trauma and numbing of general responsiveness (not present before the trauma), as indicated by three (or more) of the following:

1. efforts to avoid thoughts, feelings, or conversations associated with the trauma

2. efforts to avoid activities, places, or people that arouse recollections of the trauma

3. inability to recall an important aspect of the trauma

4. markedly diminished interest or participation in significant activities

5. feeling of detachment or estrangement from others

(Continued on Page 13)

flashback episode — *a dissociative state in which an individual feels as if he or she is reliving a traumatic event*

physiological reactivity — *quickening of the heart rate, blood pressure, and breathing resulting from exposure to internal or external cues that symbolize or resemble an aspect of the traumatic event*

(DSM-IV Criteria for PTSD, Continued)

      6. restricted range of affect (e.g., unable to have loving feelings)

      7. sense of a foreshortened future (e.g., does not expect to have a career, marriage, children, or a normal life span)

  D. Persistent symptoms of increased arousal (not present before the trauma), as indicated by two (or more) of the following:

      1. difficulty falling or staying asleep

      2. irritability or outbursts of anger

      3. difficulty concentrating

      4. hypervigilance

      5. exaggerated startle response

  E. Duration of the disturbance (symptoms in Criteria B, C, and D) is more than one month.

  F. The disturbance causes clinically significant distress or impairment in social, occupation, or other important areas of functioning.

Specify:
  Acute: if duration of symptoms is less than 3 months
  Chronic: if duration of symptoms is 3 months or more

Specify:
  With delayed onset: if onset of symptoms is at least six months after the stressor

---

The following in-depth case history of Mary T. illustrates PTSD symptom clusters as well as how a traumatized person may exhibit most, if not all, of:

Reexperiencing Symptoms (Criterion B) — Diagnosis requires a single symptom.

Avoidant/Numbing Symptoms (Criterion C) — Three symptoms required for diagnosis.

Hyperarousal Symptoms (Criterion D) — Two symptoms required for diagnosis.

■ ■ ■ ■ ■ ■ ■ ■ ■ ■ ■ ■ ■ ■ *Traumatic Event — Criterion A*

Mary T. was a 27-year-old, happily married woman. One Sunday, while driving to church, her car was hit by a semi-tractor-trailer unable to stop at a red light due to faulty brakes. As the truck crashed into the right side of the car, Mary's husband was killed instantly. Mary was badly bruised but not seriously injured. Instead, she was trapped in the car for several hours before she could be extricated. During that period, her dead husband was crushed against her. She was covered with his blood. It was a terrifying and horrifying experience. She recalls an overwhelming sense of loss, despair, and rage as she was trapped in the car waiting to be released but not wanting the separation from her husband that she knew would be her last.

Reexperiencing Symptoms — Criterion B

After a six-week convalescence with her sister in a different city, she returned to her home determined to pick up the pieces and go on with her career as a software designer in a very successful computer firm. Though extremely difficult, Mary felt that familiar surroundings, supportive colleagues, and work she had always enjoyed would provide a much-needed distraction from the *intrusive recollections* exemplified by the incessant replay in her mind of the most awful moments of the accident. However, she couldn't get her mind to focus on anything but different images from the crash: the noise of the truck, the green traffic light and the impact of her husband's limp body. She often awoke at night in a state of panic from the same *traumatic nightmare* in which she was crushed by her husband's body, drowning in his blood, and clawing at the shattered window in her attempt to escape from the car. Most disturbing were the *PTSD flashbacks,* which generally occurred when a large truck would rumble close by, especially when she was riding in a car. At such times, she would actually "see" the truck change direction and head straight towards her. On some level, she knew that her mind was playing tricks on her and that there was no truck swerving inexorably in her direction. But during these episodes, her terror was so great and her hold on reality so weak, that she could think of nothing but escape from the oncoming truck that she believed was going to destroy her.

intrusive recollections —
Criterion B_1

traumatic nightmare —
Criterion B_2

PTSD flashbacks —
Criterion B_3

With PTSD, some or all of the reexperiencing symptoms illustrate how the traumatic event remains, sometimes for decades, a dominating psychological experience, evoking panic, terror, dread, grief, or despair.

Many different kinds of stimuli intensely affected Mary: driving a car, being in close proximity to large trucks, seeing the intersection where the accident had occurred, and watching any media depiction of a motor vehicle accident. When exposed to such stimuli, she:

- **Experienced intense psychological distress** marked by terror, horror, and an overwhelming sense of loss, despair, and rage.

  experienced intense psychological distress — Criterion B_4

- **Experienced physiological reactivity** marked by a pounding heart, racing pulse, rapid breathing, sweating, and an awful headache.

  experienced physiological reactivity — Criterion B_5

Avoidant/Numbing Symptoms — Criterion C

Thoughts and memories about the accident evoked such an intense emotional and *physiological reaction*, that Mary made concerted *efforts to avoid thoughts, feelings or conversations about the trauma*. Because she didn't want to think about the accident, Mary refused to take legal action against the trucking company that had negligently failed to inspect and repair the faulty truck brakes that led to the death of her husband and her suffering. When she found herself involuntarily beginning to think about the accident, she would try to distract herself with music, work, or some other emotionally neutral matter. Mary also made a specific *effort to avoid activities, places, or people associated with the trauma*. She quit riding in the car and watching TV or movies for fear that they would contain crash scenes or other images that would remind her of the accident. She even tried to stay awake as long as she could at night to avoid the traumatic nightmares that terrified her three or four times each week.

efforts to avoid thoughts, feelings or conversations about the trauma — Criterion C_1

efforts to avoid activities, places, or people associated with the trauma — Criterion C_2

Initially, Mary was certain that she could completely recall the event. After all, her problem was not amnesia, but rather that the intrusive recollections and other reexperiencing symptoms were so terribly unbearable that she couldn't work, sleep, or function as she had before the accident. However, after weeks of reviewing and reprocessing the event with her psychotherapist, she began to remember more and more details of the accident.

inability to recall an important aspect of the trauma — *Criterion C$_3$*

The inability to recall important aspects of the trauma (psychogenic amnesia), which may last for years, is really a dissociative symptom that differs qualitatively from behavioral avoidance or psychic numbing.

diminished interest and stopped participating in social activities — *Criterion C$_4$*

detached and estranged from others — *Criterion C$_5$*

restricted range of affect — *Criterion C$_6$*

foreshortened future — *Criterion C$_7$*

difficulty falling or staying asleep — *Criterion D$_1$*

She indeed had experienced an *inability to recall an important aspect of the trauma*. What she began to recall was even worse than what she had initially remembered. She began to vividly recall the initial impact when the nose of the truck plowed through the door, sweeping her husband into her lap. Worst still, she now recalled that he didn't die instantly, but lived long enough to gaze at her imploringly, his face contorted by pain, breathing his last, and begging for help. This was the most unbearable memory of all.

Mary felt that she had become a very different person since the accident and she didn't like the changes she perceived in herself. Previously, she had been open, emotional, adventurous, and gregarious. Now, she was withdrawn, unresponsive, and solitary. She exhibited *diminished interest and stopped participating in the many social, athletic, and church activities* she previously enjoyed. She felt *detached and estranged from others*, especially from her sister and two closest friends. Part of this estrangement came from her conviction that no one could possibly know or understand how her old self had been irreversibly changed by the accident. Additionally, she felt numb, wooden, and hollow inside as if her capacity for emotional experience and expression had been completely anesthetized. This *restricted range of affect* made it impossible for her to enjoy companionship or to reciprocate feelings of warmth, friendship, intimacy or love. Finally, she felt that her life was over and that she had a *foreshortened future* with neither a career, marriage, children, or normal life span to look forward to.

Hyperarousal Symptoms — Criterion D

Mary was in a state of constant arousal, agitation, and anxiety. Others perceived her as being jumpy, nervous, easily upset, and having a hair-trigger temper. She had *difficulty falling or staying asleep* either because she couldn't distract her mind from intrusive recollections of the trauma, she was awakened by traumatic nightmares, or her high level of physiologic overdrive prohibited sleep. She exhibited *irritability or outbursts of anger* that astonished friends who had previously regarded her as an easy-going and resilient individual with a great sense of humor. She had *difficulty concentrating* either because her mind was preoccupied with intrusive recollections of the trauma, or her arousal level was so high that she could not focus on any intellectual task for a sustained period. This concentration problem forced her to take a leave of absence from her job.

Mary became obsessed with fears about personal safety, *hypervigilant* for the first sign of danger. This was especially noticeable when she was in a car, but it also manifested itself by a reluctance to go shopping by herself, a refusal to venture out of her house after dark, and her installation of an elaborate home security system. Finally, she was extremely jumpy and would exhibit an *exaggerated startle response* to any unexpected noise.

irritability or outbursts of anger — Criterion D_2

difficulty concentrating — Criterion D_3

hypervigilant — Criterion D_4

exaggerated startle response — Criterion D_5

Similarities and Differences Between PTSD & ASD

Since PTSD cannot be diagnosed until one month after the traumatic event, the diagnosis Acute Stress Disorder (ASD) was added to the DSM-IV for people who exhibit symptoms within the first few weeks, immediately after exposure to a trauma. The four primary similarities and differences between PTSD and ASD include:

1. Emphasis on Dissociative Symptoms — One must have three of the following five dissociative symptoms present to diagnose ASD. It is the inclusion and prominence of dissociative symptoms that sets ASD distinctly apart from PTSD. Two dissociative symptoms come from the PTSD cluster of Numbing Symptoms while the other three symptoms are unique to ASD:

- **Numbing (PTSD Criteria C_4-C_6)** — This is a subjective sense of numbing, detachment or absence of emotional responsiveness.

- **Dissociative Amnesia (PTSD Criterion C_3)** — This is the inability to recall an important aspect of the trauma.

Mary's PTSD symptoms persisted much longer than one month; therefore, they met the Duration (E) Criterion. It is chronic PTSD because her symptoms persisted much longer than three months.

Mary's PTSD caused clinically significant distress and impairment socially (e.g., withdrawal from friends, relationships, and activities), occupationally (i.e.., a leave of absence from work because of her inability to function), and in other important areas of functioning. Therefore, she met Functional Impairment (F) Criterion.

Empirical justification for including these three dissociative symptoms for ASD is sparse. It relies mostly on clinical observations and on evidence that people who experience acute dissociative symptoms during the traumatic event are at greater risk for the later development of PTSD.

derealization — *"An alteration in the perception or experience of the external world so that it seems strange or unreal (e.g., people may seem unfamiliar or mechanical; time may seem speeded up or slowed down)." 3 (pg. 766)*

depersonalization — *"An alteration in the perception or experience of the self so that one feels detached from, and as if one is an outside observer of one's mental processes or body (e.g., feeling like one is in a dream)." 3 (pg. 766)*

- **Reduction in Awareness** — This lack of attention or responsivity to the immediate environment makes it appear to an onlooker that the individual is "in a daze," "spaced-out," or in a world of his/her own.

- *Derealization* — The world one has always known is dramatically changed and one feels estranged or detached from the environment or has a sense that the environment is unreal. For example, feeling that places seem unfamiliar, even though one has visited them frequently in the course of one's daily routine.

- *Depersonalization* — Depersonalization may manifest itself as a distorted perception of one's body, one's identity, or one's self as a coherent entity. For example, having an out-of-body experience in which one has the experience of looking down on one's body from above; or feeling that one's body is split into sections: one part might be numb, another warm, and another cold.

2. Number of Symptoms Needed to Make a Diagnosis — While the definition of most symptoms are the same for PTSD and ASD, the number of symptoms a person experiences before meeting the diagnostic criteria is different. Only one reexperiencing, avoidant, or anxiety/arousal symptom must be present to meet ASD diagnostic criteria.

3. Definition of Clinically Significant Distress or Functional Impairment — This is essentially the same as the PTSD Functional Impairment, F, Criterion. For the ASD diagnosis, the definition of functional impairment now stipulates that a person is functionally impaired if s/he cannot obtain "necessary assistance" or cannot mobilize "personal resources" by telling family members about the traumatic experience.

4. Onset and Duration of Symptoms — ASD must last a minimum of two days and a maximum of four weeks; PTSD cannot be diagnosed until at least four weeks after the traumatic experience.

What Tools are Available for Clinical Assessment?

For clinicians assessing PTSD, there are a variety of structured interview and self-report instruments that can be used in conjunction with the clinical interview. This section provides important guidance about conducting clinical interviews with those suffering from PTSD as well as a brief overview of available instruments and their use. Appendices A & B provide detailed information on these structured interviews and self-report instruments.

The Clinical Interview

Diagnosing PTSD can take several meetings where the clinician carefully conducts an interview, asking questions on risk factors for PTSD and ruling out other possible disorders. Additionally, assessment tools such as structured interviews or *psychometric instruments* may be utilized.

General Considerations

In general, PTSD is not a difficult diagnosis to make if the clinician keeps the diagnostic criteria in mind. However, it is essential that clinicians conduct the diagnostic interview in a manner that acknowledges the client's worst fears and in an environment of sensitivity, safety, and trust. The clinician is asking the client to take a tremendous risk and abandon the avoidance behaviors, protective strategies, and other psychological strategies that currently buffer the client from experiencing intolerable memories and feelings associated with the traumatic event. In the case of chronic PTSD, where such protective layers have solidified for years or decades, clinicians must be patient and obtain the trauma history at a pace that clients can tolerate. It is usually helpful if clinicians immediately communicate that they recognize how difficult it must be for clients to answer these questions. It is also helpful for clinicians to ask clients to let them know when the interview has become too upsetting and to back off immediately when a client says that it is so.

The caution, sensitivity, and patience, needed with respect to the PTSD diagnostic interview, also must be evident to the client with ASD. The major difference, of course, is that PTSD clients have a chronic condition to which they have had an opportunity to adapt whereas ASD clients have been acutely traumatized and, therefore, find themselves in an intense, novel and extremely disturbing psychological state that they usually cannot comprehend. They may feel that they are out of control and/or losing their minds. Such clients may exhibit severe anxiety, agitation, and apprehension. Therefore, when conducting an ASD assessment, clinicians must initially approach it as carefully and thoughtfully as they would any other urgent or emergent psychiatric evaluation. By exhibiting

psychometric instruments — tests which measure psychological factors such as personality, intelligence, beliefs, fears

clinical behavior that communicates patience, sensitivity, and competence, clinicians can usually obtain a thorough diagnostic assessment from the most anxious, avoidant, and hypervigilant client.

Risk Factors

There is little empirical data on risk factors for ASD. A reasonable guess is that risk factors for PTSD (as listed in Figure 2.4) might be expected to similarly affect vulnerability to ASD. Indeed, in one study it was found that female gender, stress severity, depression, and an avoidant coping style were risk factors for ASD.[15] As noted earlier, ASD itself appears to be a risk factor for the later development of PTSD.[11-12]

Since most people who are traumatized do not develop PTSD, it is important to know who might be at a greater risk for the disorder. Some believe that traumatized people who develop PTSD have specific preexisting psychological and/or biological abnormalities that make them more vulnerable to PTSD than others.[16] The factors listed in Figure 2.4 are associated with the greatest risk for PTSD.[17]

Self-report Instruments and Structured Interviews

Many structured interviews and questionnaires have been developed for assessing and diagnosing PTSD, some have clinical use while others are used primarily for research purposes. These instruments, reviewed in detail in appendices A and B, fall into three overlapping categories:

1. **Trauma Exposure Scales** are used to determine whether an individual has been exposed to a Criterion A_1 event. These questionnaires document the nature and severity of overwhelming stressors. General exposure questionnaires inquire about exposure to all possible kinds of catastrophic events while specific exposure scales focus on a specific kind of traumatic experience such as: child abuse, domestic violence, rape, combat exposure, or torture.

For a detailed review of how the instruments in these categories can be used with adults and children, see appendices A and B on pages 79-90.

2. **Diagnostic Instruments** are either structured clinical interviews administered by a clinician or lay interviews designed for survey research. These are often broad spectrum instruments that inquire about all DSM-IV diagnoses with a separate specific module dedicated to PTSD

Figure 2.4 — Risk Factors for PTSD		
Pre-Traumatic Risk Factors	**Traumatic Risk Factors**	**Post-Traumatic Risk Factors**
*Gender — Women are twice as likely as men to develop PTSD at some point in their lives. **Age** —Young adults under 25 **Education** — Those without a college education **Childhood Trauma** — Those who experienced sexual abuse as children, for example **Childhood Adversity** — Those who experienced economic deprivation or parental separation/divorce before age 10, for example **Previous Exposure to Child Trauma** — Those who experienced child abuse, rape, war, or motor vehicle accidents as children, for example **Prior Psychiatric disorder** (of any kind) **Childhood Attention Deficit Hyperactivity Disorder** *Personality Pathology* **Exposure to Trauma as an Adult** **Adverse Life Events** — Those who experienced divorce, loss of job, failure at school, for example **Poor Physical Health and Financial Problems** — Those who experienced serious debt or a sudden financial setback, for example **Family History of Psychiatric Disorders** ****Genetic Vulnerability/Personal Resilience** — Research indicates a possible genetic tendency toward development of PTSD following exposure to trauma; conversely a similar tendency toward cognitive and emotional resilience promotes recovery from the impact of trauma.	**Severity ("dose") of the trauma** — The greater the magnitude of trauma exposure, the greater the likelihood of PTSD. The most severe traumas often include perceived life threat or serious injury. **Nature of the Trauma** — Interpersonal violence (e.g., rape, physical attack, torture, war-zone trauma) in which there is a human perpetrator is much more likely to produce PTSD than an impersonal event (e.g., a natural disaster). **Participation in Atrocities (either as a perpetrator or witness)** — Vietnam and other military veterans have a greater risk factor.	**Poor Social Support** **Development of ASD** as a risk factor is currently the subject of research. **Immediate Traumatic/Post-Traumatic Reaction** — such as *peritraumatic dissociation,* physiological arousal, or avoidant/numbing symptoms — are all currently under investigation as possible risk factors for PTSD.

personality pathology — *maladaptive pattern of relating to other people that severely impairs social functioning and adaptive potential*

peritraumatic dissociation — *dissociation during and shortly after the trauma*

*One reason why females are more likely to develop PTSD is that they are more likely to have experienced interpersonal violence such as rape, sexual molestation, childhood parental neglect, and childhood sexual/physical abuse. Though the reasons are not understood even when the above factors are taken into consideration, women are still more likely to develop PTSD than men.

**Much current research is focused on why some people are psychologically vulnerable while others are much more resilient when confronted by the same traumatic event.

diagnostic criteria. These instruments can also be used to detect comorbid diagnoses.

3. **Symptom Severity Scales** are usually self-report questionnaires in which individuals indicate (often on a four- or five-point scale) the intensity of a specific PTSD symptom (e.g., traumatic nightmares). Within this class of instruments are structured clinical interviews that can be

used both as diagnostic instruments and symptom severity scales such as the Clinician Administered PTSD Scale (CAPS).

Most PTSD instruments have been designed for adults. They are described in appendix A. Appendix B covers PTSD questionnaires and structured interviews developed exclusively for children.

In practice, it is usually best to start with a general trauma exposure scale. If the client reports that s/he has previously been exposed to a Criterion A_1 event, one can either inquire in more detail about the specific trauma exposure (e.g., child abuse) or proceed directly to a diagnostic instrument to determine whether PTSD is present. The severity of PTSD can next be determined with a symptom severity scale or with the Clinician Administered PTSD Scale (CAPS), which helps diagnose and determine symptom severity (see appendix A).

Figure 2.5 lists these instruments by function, delineating those developed for adults from those developed for children. For detailed descriptions, review appendices A and B.

Psychometric Instruments

There are several psychometric instruments commonly used in routine comprehensive psychological assessment. With the exception of the *Minnesota Multiphasic Personality Inventory (MMPI)*, which has two specific subscales for PTSD (see Appendix A), none of these instruments has proven useful for differentiating those with PTSD from others. Although PTSD clients may exhibit abnormalities on *Millon Clinical Multiaxial Inventory (MCMI)*, *Rorschach Ink Blot Test*, or *Wechsler Adult Intelligence Scale (WAIS)*, there is nothing specific about such response profiles to recommend their use with assessing PTSD.

What Differentiates PTSD from Other Disorders?

Victims of trauma may suffer from psychiatric disorders in addition to PTSD (comorbid disorders) or their trauma may result in a disorder that is different from PTSD,[16] such as a medical disorder,[19-20] or another "unofficial" post-traumatic disorder.[21]

A thorough and comprehensive discussion of PTSD assessment can be found in a recent book devoted entirely to this topic.[18]

Minnesota Multiphasic Personality Inventory (MMPI) — a widely used instrument for mental disorders, assessing personality and symptoms of distress

Million Clinical Multiaxial Inventory (MCMI) — an instrument for assessing mental disorders, developed for use with hospitalized psychiatric clients

Rorschach Ink Blot Test — a projective measure of personality assessment that utilizes "neutral" inkblots in which the client responds to the blot with their own experiences and perceptual orientation

Wechsler Adult Intelligence Scale (WAIS) — a widely used intelligence test designed to measure a persons intellectual potential and decision making processes

Figure 2.5 — PTSD Assessment Scales

Instruments for Assessing Exposure to Trauma*	Instruments for Diagnosing PTSD	Instruments for Determining Symptom Severity
For Adults Traumatic Stress Schedule (TSS) - *general* Potential Stressor Experiences Inventory (PSEI) - *general* Traumatic Events Questionnaire (TEQ) - *general* Evaluation of Lifetime Stressors (ELS) - *general* Child Abuse and Trauma Scale - *childhood trauma* Childhood Trauma Questionnaire - *childhood trauma* Familial Experiences Inventory - *childhood trauma* Retrospective Assessment of Traumatic Experiences (RATE) - *childhood trauma* Early Trauma Inventory (ETI) - *childhood trauma* Conflict Tactics Scale (CTS) - *domestic violence* Abusive Behavior Inventory (ABI) - *domestic violence* Sexual Experiences Survey (SES) - *domestic violence* Wyatt Sex History Questionnaire (WSHQ) - *domestic violence* Combat Exposure Scale (CES) - *war-zone trauma* Women's Wartime Stressor Scale (WWSS) - *war-zone trauma* Harvard Trauma Questionnaire (HTQ) - *torture*	Structured Clinical Interview for DSM-IV (SCID): PTSD Module Clinician Administered PTSD Scale (CAPS) PTSD-Interview The Davidson Self-Rating PTSD Scale Composite International Diagnostic Interview (CIDI) Diagnostic Interview Schedule IV (DIS-IV)	PTSD Checklist (PCL) PTSD Symptom Scale (PSS) PK-Scale of the MMPI-2 PS-Scale of the MMPI-2 SCL-PTSD Impact of Event Scale–Revised (IES-R) Mississippi Scale for Combat-Related PTSD (M-PTSD) Civilian Mississippi Scale Penn Inventory Trauma Symptom Checklist–40 (TSC-40) Trauma Symptom Inventory (TSI)
For Children My Worst Experience Survey (MWES) My Worst School Experience Survey (MWSES) Traumatic Event Screening Instrument (TESI) When Bad Things Happen Scale (WBTHS) Children's Sexual Behavior Inventory 3 (CSBI-3) Child Rating Scales of Exposure to Interpersonal Abuse (CRS-EIA) Angie/Andy CRS (A/A CRS) My Exposure to Violence (My-ETV)	Diagnostic Interview for Children and Adolescents-Revised (DICA-R) Clinician Administered PTSD Scale for Children (CAPS-C) Diagnostic Interview Schedule for Children (DISC)	Child Post-Traumatic Stress Reaction Index (CPTS-RI) Child's Reaction to Traumatic Events Scale (CRTES) Children's Impact of Traumatic Events Scale (CITES) Trauma Symptom Checklist for Children (TSCC) Child Dissociative Checklist (CDC)

Comorbid Disorders

Individuals with lifetime PTSD will likely meet DSM-IV diagnostic criteria for at least one other psychiatric disorder. In fact, the National Comorbidity Survey found that approximately 80 percent of all men or women who have ever had PTSD had at least one other affective, anxiety, or chemical use/dependency disorder.[1] Common coexisting disorders with PTSD include: Major Depressive Disorder, Dysthymia, Generalized Anxiety Disorder, Simple Phobia, Social Phobia,

Traumatic exposure scales include both those developed to inquire about all types of traumatic experiences as well as those developed for specific traumas (e.g., child abuse, domestic violence, rape, war exposure, and torture). Scales listed indicate purpose in italicized type.

*comorbid disorders —
major psychiatric disorders
that are present at the
same time an individual has
full-fledged PTSD*

*Guilt, which is often seen in
depression or dysthymia is
not a diagnostic symptom
of PTSD. However, PTSD
clients will sometimes
express "survival guilt"
because they survived a war
or disaster whereas a loved
one did not.*

Panic Disorder, Alcohol Abuse/Dependence, Drug Abuse/
Dependence or Conduct Disorder. Figure 2.6 details these
findings.

One reason for the prevalence of comorbid disorders is the
symptom overlap between PTSD and other disorders. In general, if all criteria for PTSD and another disorder are met,
multiple diagnoses need to be made. Listed below are factors
that can help differentiate PTSD from other disorders.

1. **Depressed or Dysthymic clients** may exhibit insomnia,
   impaired concentration, social withdrawal, and diminished
   interest similar to PTSD. However, these affective disorders differ from PTSD because of the presence of depressed mood, weight loss, suicidal thoughts, and a slow-
   ing of thoughts and actions (e.g., "psychomotor retardation").

2. **Generalized Anxiety Disorder clients** exhibit a number
   of symptoms in common with PTSD, including:
   • Irritability
   • Hypervigilence
   • Exaggerated startle response
   • Impaired concentration
   • Insomnia
   • Autonomic hyperarousal

   What differentiates a client with Generalized Anxiety
   Disorder from one with PTSD is the presence of unrealistic worry, muscle tension, restlessness, dry mouth, frequent urination, and a lump in the throat.

3. **Phobic clients** (e.g., Simple Phobia, Social Phobia, and
   Agoraphobia) will exhibit avoidant behaviors that may be
   triggered by environmental and/or social stimuli. They
   may also exhibit PTSD arousal symptoms. The two major
   differences are that phobic clients do not exhibit PTSD
   numbing symptoms and become aroused only when they
   believe they will be exposed to the feared stimulus or
   situation. PTSD clients, on the other hand, are perpetually
   in a state of hyperarousal.

4. **Panic Disorder** resembles PTSD because panic clients
   exhibit many symptoms of autonomic hyperarousal and
   may exhibit dissociation. In contrast to PTSD, however,
   panic attacks are unexpected and occur spontaneously,
   they are associated with symptoms of choking, numbness,
   tingling, fear of going crazy, and fear of dying.

5. **Chemical Abuse/Dependency** often appears in PTSD clients as a comorbid diagnosis. However, the PTSD diagnostic criteria address no symptoms concerning use and misuse of alcohol or drugs.

6. **Conduct Disorder** is associated with frequent acts of physical aggression and criminal behavior. PTSD clients' irritability, aggression, and illegal behaviors are not considered diagnostic symptoms.

Figure 2.6 — DSM-IV Disorders Frequently Comorbid with PTSD

from the National Comorbidity Survey[1]

Diagnosis	Lifetime Prevalence	Remarks
Major Depressive Disorder	48%	
Dysthymia	22%	
Generalized Anxiety Disorder	16%	
Simple Phobia	30%	
Social Phobia	28%	
Panic Disorder	12.6% vs. 7.3%	women>men
Agoraphobia	22.4% vs. 16.1%	women>men
Alcohol Abuse/Dependence	51.9% vs. 27.9%	men>women
Drug Abuse/Dependence	34.5% vs. 26.9%	men>women
Conduct Disorder	43.3% vs. 15.4%	men>women

Medical Disorders

Growing evidence indicates that exposure to catastrophic events is a risk factor for many medical disorders affecting the cardiovascular, gastrointestinal, endocrinological, musculoskeletal, and other bodily systems.[19-20]

Other "Unofficial" Post-Traumatic Syndromes

Prolonged trauma, especially childhood sexual abuse or torture during political incarceration, may produce a clinical syndrome that differs considerably from that seen in PTSD. This syndrome, provisionally called "complex PTSD," features:[21]

- Impulsivity
- Dissociation
- *Somatization*

It is possible that PTSD mediates medical problems because the disruption in major bodily systems associated with PTSD (such as the cardiovascular, hormonal or immunological systems) would be expected to jeopardize health, but research on this question is at a very preliminary stage.[19-20]

somatization *— the expression of emotional distress through physical symptoms such as peptic ulcer, asthma, or chronic pain*

affective lability — *rapid and unpredictable shifts in mood state*

pathological changes — *changes resulting in an abnormal condition that prevents proper psychological functioning*

- *Affective lability*
- Interpersonal difficulties
- *Pathological changes* in personal identity (e.g. Dissociative Identity Disorder)

Therapy Notes from the Desk of Pat Owen

June 18

Completed assessment of Mary T. Obviously meets criteria for PTSD. She hyperventilated and became agitated, tearful, and unable to speak when pressed for details about the accident. She however, provided enough information on current symptoms to diagnose PTSD including: a sense of helplessness and horror, intrusive recollections, nightmares of accident, emotional/ physiological reactions exhibited during interview in response to my questions, avoidance of thought about accident by playing radio/TV as distraction, avoidance of riding in a car if possible, diminished interest in church and sports, detachment: avoiding friends and social situations, restricted affect — reports no feelings, "like a robot," can't concentrate, insomnia, irritability, hypervigilent and startle response.

Assessment:
- Clearly has severe case of PTSD
- Need to evaluate comorbid diagnoses
- Not sure what treatment she can tolerate

Chapter Three: Psychological Treatments for PTSD

Diary of Mary T.

July 2

Had my fifth session of exposure treatment today. It's hard to admit how scared I was at first. After all, Dr. Owen wanted me to imagine I was back in the car and to go through the whole accident detail by detail. I really was terrified and sure that I'd fall apart. But she was patient. Didn't rush me. And backed off when I started to lose It. Before I knew it, I could really let myself begin to remember what happened. And the more I did it, the easier it got, and the less upset I became.

I'm not there yet. It's still very painful to keep bringing back all that stuff about the accident. But I am getting stronger, and I have another five sessions to go.

This chapter answers the following:

- **What are the Global Treatment Issues Related to PTSD?** — This section addresses the unique PTSD treatment issues involving why help is sought at a particular time, what other problems may need to be dealt with before treating the PTSD, and how clinicians can maintain a healthy, productive relationship with the client and his/her traumatic situation.

- **What Psychological Treatments are Available for Adults with PTSD?** — This section covers the nature and efficacy of global therapies, individual therapies, family/marriage therapies, group therapies, and social/rehabilitative therapies.

- **What Psychological Treatments are Available for Children and Adolescents with PTSD, and How Effective Are Those Treatments?** — This section discusses how developmental stages impact treatments selected as well as defining what treatments seem most effective.

What are the Global Treatment Issues Related to PTSD?

After you have determined that a client requesting treatment does have PTSD, there are a number of clinical questions that need to be addressed. In most respects, these questions are no different than with other psychiatric disorders, although the presence of PTSD sometimes raises unique variations on these themes, such as:

- Why is Help Sought Now?

- Is Treating PTSD the First Order of Business?

- What General Issues Must be Considered When Choosing a Specific Treatment Option?

- What are the Major Personal Issues for Clinicians When Treating Someone with PTSD?

Why is Help Sought Now?

When an individual complains of the recent onset of reexperiencing, avoidant/numbing, or hyperarousal symptoms, it is usually pretty obvious why they are seeking treatment at this time and that PTSD is the first (and possibly only) order of business. On the other hand, when a person with chronic PTSD for many years suddenly requests treatment, it is usually because something has changed abruptly in their lives. This change has disrupted the equilibrium they had achieved both in terms of coping with PTSD symptoms and with the demands of family, friends, work, and society.

Sometimes the precipitant is obvious. For example:

- A woman who was raped many years ago was recently sexually harassed or threatened.

- A combat veteran, who now works as a policeman, has had his partner seriously wounded in a gunfight or thought he might be killed himself in the same encounter.

Sometimes the clinician must take a careful history to identify the recent precipitant. For example:

- A Red Cross disaster worker complains of traumatic nightmares related to an event s/he hadn't thought about for a long time. It is likely that certain specific details of a recent disaster reactivated memories of a similar event in the past, about which there remain intense, unresolved emotional feelings.

- A woman who has successfully dealt with the emotional consequences of her own childhood sexual abuse begins having intrusive recollections of this traumatic experience when her adolescent daughter begins dating or becomes sexually active.

- A military veteran may experience a reexacerbation of symptoms when television coverage focuses on new military offensives (e.g., Persian Gulf, Bosnia, Somalia, etc.) or when his child is called up for military duty.

- For older veterans, the death of an adult child (even by natural causes such as cancer) may reactivate survival guilt about having outlived buddies at Normandy Beach or in Vietnam.

Some trauma-related stimuli can be very disguised. For example, PTSD symptoms may suddenly occur in a successful business woman (with a *well-encapsulated* sexual trauma history that has never caused emotional difficulty before) who feels that her professional advancement has been unfairly and consistently blocked by hostile or oppressive male superiors against whom she feels powerless. Although the precipitating stressor is in the workplace, her nightmares are inexplicably (to her) about the sexual abuse she suffered decades earlier.

well-encapsulated — *psychological buffers that prevent a person from experiencing a painful situation, such as refusing to read newspaper accounts of sexual abuse*

Is Treating PTSD the First Order of Business?

In all the examples just cited, PTSD is clearly the first order of business, and the clinician must develop a treatment plan that addresses both the current precipitant as well as unresolved past traumatic issues that have become central to the current clinical problem.

Sometimes, however, PTSD may not be the first order of business because other clinical issues must take priority before PTSD treatment can be initiated. Common reasons for delaying PTSD treatment include:

- There is a psychiatric emergency.
- There is serious alcohol or drug abuse/dependence.
- A comorbid disorder must be attended to first.
- There is a marital/familial/workplace crisis that demands immediate attention.

Psychiatric Emergency

When clients with PTSD are suicidal, homicidal, or otherwise so out of control that they need the safety, structure, and control of an inpatient hospital setting, they must be hospitalized without delay. A discharge plan can be developed that will implement PTSD treatment along with other necessary measures when these clients are ready to leave the hospital.

Alcohol or Drug Abuse/Dependence

It is a waste of time to initiate PTSD treatment for someone who is too caught up in the addiction intoxication/withdrawal cycle to participate meaningfully in any psychotherapeutic initiative. Many clinicians refuse work with clients if they come to appointments intoxicated or if they are unable to work in psychotherapy because of their alcohol or drug abuse/dependency. If the chemical abuse/dependency is severely

Clinicians must recognize that PTSD symptoms may worsen after detoxification, and help clients prepare for this serious change.

It is essential to begin PTSD treatment as early in the detoxification or rehabilitation phase as possible to minimize the impact of the predictable exacerbation of reexperiencing and hyperarousal symptoms. There are many examples, unfortunately, of recently detoxified clients who relapsed and resumed their previous chemical misuse without such preparation.[22]

The best approach in a professional treatment program is one in which the staff attends to both the alcohol/drug misuse and the PTSD simultaneously.[22]

Ideally, one would hope to initiate treatment simultaneously for both PTSD and the comorbid disorder but, when this is impossible and when the comorbid disorder is more severe, PTSD treatment is not the first order of business.

disruptive, they may need to undergo inpatient detoxification and post-detoxification alcohol or drug rehabilitation (that often includes a commitment to attend Alcoholics Anonymous or Narcotics Anonymous meetings).

When clients agree to such a treatment approach, there are some serious potential dangers against which the clinician must prepare and protect his or her client; specifically, the fantasy that once sobriety has been achieved, all will be well. This fantasy is understandable, since it takes a great deal of determination and discomfort to kick a habit that has dominated one's life. In addition, some drug rehabilitation and Peer Counseling approaches strongly reinforce this erroneous belief. Sadly, the opposite is sometimes the case with PTSD clients. This is because alcohol and (prescription or illicit) drug abuse often serve to blunt or numb intolerable PTSD reexperiencing or hyperarousal symptoms. During the acute withdrawal period within the first few days of detoxification, previous alcohol/drug-suppressed PTSD symptoms come raging to the forefront of conscious awareness.[23] More importantly, the PTSD client who has successfully undergone detoxification is now suddenly thrust into the world without this protection.

Co-Existing Psychiatric Disorders

Because 80 percent of people who ever have PTSD will have at least one other psychiatric disorder during their lives, sometimes the severity of the comorbid disorder demands initial attention (see chapter 2, pages 23-25). For example, a severely depressed individual (with comorbid PTSD) who may not need to be hospitalized may still need aggressive depression treatment before PTSD treatment can be considered. The same holds true for people with an immobilizing panic disorder, individuals whose eating disorder has seriously compromised their health, or persons with other psychiatric problems that are currently more incapacitating or potentially dangerous than the PTSD.

Situational Factors

Some family, vocational, or environmental situations may require intervention before addressing PTSD. For example:

• A women whose PTSD is the result of ongoing domestic violence is a poor candidate for psychotherapy, especially Cognitive Behavior Therapy, as long as she remains in an abusive relationship. Here, the first order of business is providing a safe and secure living situation (e.g., a battered women's shelter or safe house).

- A marriage on the brink of collapse because of one member's PTSD symptoms needs couples therapy before starting individual therapy for the PTSD sufferer.

- An employee working in conditions perceived to be unsafe has PTSD symptoms continually stirred up by workplace conditions. The immediate challenge is to reduce incapacitating anxiety before PTSD treatment can begin. This could be accomplished by assignment to another tour of duty, by changes in the working environment, or by a medical/psychiatric leave of absence.

- Military personnel in a war zone experiencing "battle fatigue" or ASD may need to be removed from the immediate dangers of the war zone to the safety of a front echelon medical unit where they can receive appropriate intervention.

What General Issues Must be Considered When Choosing a Specific Treatment Option?

When creating a treatment plan for someone with PTSD, there are a number of factors to consider, including:

- **Combined Treatment** — To provide the best possible care for clients, different therapies are often combined (e.g., individual therapy and medications).

- **Treatment of Comorbid Disorders** — Treatments may need to be chosen that address multiple disorders at the same time.

- **Treating** *"Complex PTSD"* — For those who experienced severe trauma, a new clinical syndrome has been proposed, perhaps demanding a longer term treatment plan.[21]

- **Cross-Cultural Considerations** — Clinicians need to be sensitive to cultural differences in PTSD assessment and treatment.

- **Recovered Memories** — There is some controversy over whether or not previously forgotten traumatic memories can be recovered many years later, and how these memories should be addressed by therapists.

trauma focus treatment
— *PTSD treatments in which the client is directed to explore in depth the trauma as an avenue for healing (see page 38)*

There is no empirical data to guide us as to what combination of treatments are best. Relying on clinical experience, it is a good clinical practice to introduce only one therapeutic approach at a time and to carefully gauge its effectiveness before combining such treatment with another.

See pages 23-25 (chapter 2), and page 77-78 (chapter 4), for more detailed information on treating comorbid disorders.

fragmented thoughts —
the inability to sustain continuity and coherence in one's cognitive processes

amnesia — *mental syndrome characterized by partial or complete memory loss*

Combined Treatment

When combining treatment methods, clinicians most commonly add pharmacotherapy to individual or group psychotherapy. For example, drug treatment may not only ameliorate psychobiological abnormalities associated with PTSD but may provide sufficient anxiety reduction for clients to participate in *trauma focus treatment* including Exposure Therapy (see page 46). Another common combination is individual treatment plus marital/family therapy, which addresses interpersonal problems associated with PTSD.

Treatment of Comorbid Disorders

The preferred treatment may be one that targets symptoms for both the PTSD and comorbid disorder simultaneously.

"Complex PTSD"

Many clinicians who work with victims of prolonged trauma, such as incest and torture, argue that these clients suffer from a clinical syndrome, named "Complex PTSD", that is not adequately characterized by the current PTSD construct.[21] The non-PTSD symptoms that comprise Complex PTSD include:

- **Behavioral difficulties** (e.g., impulsivity, aggression, sexual acting out, eating disorders, alcohol/drug abuse, and self-destructive actions)

- **Emotional difficulties** (e.g., affective lability, rage, depression, and panic)

- **Cognitive difficulties** (e.g., *fragmented thoughts*, dissociation, and *amnesia*) .

Proponents of the Complex PTSD construct suggest that its treatment usually requires long-term individual and group therapies, focusing on family function, vocational rehabilitation, social skills training, and alcohol/drug rehabilitation.[21, 24]

The validity of Complex PTSD as a unique diagnostic entity is controversial. Many PTSD experts point out that the vast majority of clients with Complex PTSD have already met diagnostic criteria for PTSD, and an alternate diagnosis of Complex PTSD is superfluous and has little scientific support. This controversy has precluded Complex PTSD from being included in the DSM-IV.

Cross-Cultural Considerations

PTSD has been criticized from a cross-cultural perspective as a Euroamerican construct that fails to take into account culture-specific causes of stress that might be seen in trauma survivors from more traditional cultures. Some symptoms fall outside strict DSM-IV diagnostic criteria but appear to be dramatic indications of clinically significant post-traumatic distress in their own right.[25] For example, in Latin America, people are diagnosed with *"calor"* and *"ataques de nervios."*

Clinicians need to be attuned to such culture-specific idioms of distress so that they can identify post-traumatic distress when appropriate. It is also essential that, having made the diagnosis, clinicians initiate a culturally sensitive variant of PTSD treatment that will work. For example, an egalitarian approach to family therapy is incomprehensible in some cultures where the father holds a position of authority that cannot be challenged. Likewise, clinicians pressuring for overt discussion of sexual trauma by unmarried Islamic women in group therapy fail to recognize the shameful and potentially socially disastrous consequences of such disclosure.

Recovered Memories

There is a controversy as to whether or not a person can recover trauma memories many years after the trauma occurred.[26] Adults who had been sexually assaulted as children sometimes have no memories of these childhood assaults.[27] Sometimes, such missing traumatic memories later become accessible so that clients then recall traumatic childhood events such as father-daughter incest.[26, 31]

The accuracy and validity of such recovered memories has been emphatically challenged and called the "false memory syndrome" by these researchers and accused perpetrators because of the fallibility and difficulty authenticating such "rediscovered, previously repressed" memories.[32-35] Some argue that many of these recalled memories are suggested by therapists and therefore actually manufactured during the course of psychotherapy.

In some cases, there is irrefutable evidence that such childhood sexual abuse actually occurred among women who were sexually assaulted during childhood (documented by recorded visits to hospital emergency rooms), but were sometimes unable to recall that traumatic event until many years later.[26]

Marsella, Friedman, Kinzie, Gusman, and Stamm each offer good discussions of culturally sensitive treatment for trauma survivors.[25, 28-30]

"calor" — a stress-related syndrome observed among Salvadoran women described as a surge of intense heat that may rapidly spread throughout the entire body for a few moments or for several days

"ataques de nervios" — a common symptom of distress among Hispanic American groups involving anxiety, uncontrollable shouting and crying, trembling, heart palpitations, difficulty moving limbs, difficulty breathing, dizziness, fainting spells, and dissociative symptoms such as amnesia and alteration of consciousness

Clinicians need to familiarize themselves with the complexity, fallibility, and reconstructive nature of human memory.[26]

However, some researchers have reported that there is adequate proof of a few cases in which traumatic memories were forgotten and later "recovered," but it is unknown whether or not this is an extremely rare event.[32, 36] Additionally, it has been reported that validated "recovered" memories have been triggered spontaneously by life events that resembled the initial trauma in some significant way rather than by psychotherapy.[26, 36-37] Such a scenario is entirely consistent with a conditioning model of PTSD in which pertinent stimuli can evoke trauma-related thoughts, feelings, or behavior.

Though this issue remains controversial, there is general agreement that:

- Memory, especially childhood memory, is fallible but not necessarily incorrect.

- Documented traumatic events are sometimes forgotten.

- Forgotten memories of documented traumatic events are sometimes "recovered." [26-27, 31-33, 36-39]

According to a recent report published by the International Society for Traumatic Stress Studies, "Professionals agree that there is no standard procedure for establishing the accuracy of recovered memories in individual cases and that in clinical practice, it is up to the client to come to his or her own conclusions about whether or not he or she was previously traumatized and about the specific details of such events. Clinicians should convey to clients the fallibility of memories and should avoid overly aggressive techniques such as suggesting to clients that they 'must have had' a traumatic experience (based entirely on reports of symptoms) when clients have no recollection that such an event ever occurred. Professionals also agree that it is not the role of clinicians to instruct or pressure clients to take a particular (legal) course of action with accused offenders and/or family members during the course of therapy for childhood abuse." [26 (p. 23-24)]

What are the Major Personal Issues for Clinicians When Treating Someone with PTSD?

Clinicians treating individuals with PTSD must deal with the personal impact client reports of human suffering have on them personally. Specific issues to note include:

- **Therapeutic Neutrality vs. Advocacy** – Clinicians often wish to engage in activities to help prevent catastrophes in the future.

- *Vicarious Traumatization* – Clinicians sometimes experience strong emotions in response to hearing a client's story of trauma.

- *Countertransference* – A client's experience of trauma may remind the clinician of personal traumatic experiences. The feelings and behaviors resulting from these memories must be carefully managed.

- **Clinician Self-Care** – Work with trauma victims is intense and taxing for clinicians. Strategies for self-care are crucial.

vicarious traumatization — *feelings, personal distress, and symptoms that are sometimes evoked in clinicians who work with PTSD clients*

countertransference — *the clinician's psychological reaction to something the client said or did*

Therapeutic Neutrality vs. Advocacy

Trauma work challenges the traditional psychotherapeutic principle that the clinician must remain neutral, because so many people seeking help have suffered from abusive violence, state-sponsored terrorism, or other man-made catastrophes. It is only natural that clinicians feelings about such injustices are mobilized and channeled into advocacy activities to prevent such human suffering in the future. However, advocacy can undermine therapy.[40] For example, the clinician should never assume the role of rescuer for a specific client. When a clinician intervenes directly to confront a problem that the client seems unable to address, it implies that the client cannot cope with problems without assistance. The more the clinician's words and deeds suggest that the client is helpless, the more disempowered the client becomes. Such clinician behavior perpetuates client beliefs about being personally incompetent and that the world is overwhelming.

While we feel compassion for our clients and outrage at what caused their PTSD, we cannot abandon or forfeit our clinical skills because of our private stance as advocates.

However, clinicians can and should act as advocates for clients in obtaining those services requiring a professional referral. Such advocacy might include dealing with local, state, or federal agencies in order to gain access to community support or victim assistance programs.[41]

Vicarious Traumatization

Working with clients who have suffered trauma is difficult. Clients' powerful stories often generate intense emotions within clinicians, who may despair because they are powerless to protect clients (especially children) or feel guilty that they were not personally exposed to such horrors. Additionally,

Vicarious traumatization can cause severe personal distress among clinicians, and it can impair their professional judgment and performance.

clinicians may become so overwhelmed by the traumatic experiences reported by their clients that they have intrusive recollection and nightmares about such material. Feelings such as these can produce a number of inappropriate behaviors (e.g., numbing behavior, attempts to rescue the client, and minimization or avoidance of traumatic material), that compromise therapy or may even disturb the clinician on a personal level. This process has been labeled "vicarious traumatization" and "compassion fatigue." [42-43]

Countertransference

Since more than half of all American men and women will be exposed to at least one traumatic event during their lives, it is likely that many mental health professionals will also have been traumatized — among whom, some will undoubtedly have developed PTSD.[1]

Countertransference, a psychoanalytic term, refers to personal memories and feelings elicited from the clinician by the client in the course of therapy. Whereas vicarious traumatization refers to a psychological response that might occur among clinicians who have never been traumatized themselves, countertransference applies to situations in which client material triggers intrusive recollections in the clinicians of their own traumatic or other significant personal experiences.

Countertransference most likely occurs when the similarities between client and clinician experiences are sufficient to trigger the clinician's intrusive recollections, avoidant/numbing, or hyperarousal symptoms as well as other intrapsychic and interpersonal issues.

More information on PTSD countertransference can be found in authoritative sources such as Herman, Danieli, or Wilson.[40, 44-45]

An important variation on this theme is the countertransference that occurs when clinicians themselves are attempting to cope with the same catastrophic stresses as their clientele. For example, clinicians working in a war-zone or natural disaster area are also personally affected by the catastrophic stresses for which their clients seek treatment. Under such circumstances, it is suggested that clinicians receive *Psychological Debriefing* or more extensive attention for their own post-traumatic distress if they expect to be able to help others.

Psychological Debriefing — an intervention conducted by trained professionals shortly after a catastrophe, allowing victims to talk about their experience and receive information on "normal" types of reactions to such an event

Clinician Self-Care

Whether due to vicarious traumatization or countertransference, disturbing feelings and thoughts can impair both the personal mental health and the professional performance of clinicians treating individuals with PTSD. Clinicians may find themselves trapped in a vicious cycle in which the more symptomatic, maladaptive, and ineffective they become, the more they minimize this state of affairs and plunge themselves into their work. Unfortunately, under such circumstances clinicians most desperately need (but are unlikely to seek) colleague supervision or assistance.

Recognizing these occupational hazards or personal difficulties is only the first step. Clinicians must make a conscious, sustained, and systematic effort to prevent or remedy vicarious traumatization or countertransference. This can be accomplished through professional and personal self-care activities, such as:[46-48]

- Having regular supervision

- Developing a supportive environment at work

- Placing limits on case load size – especially with respect to the number of trauma cases

- Maintaining boundaries between personal and professional activities

- Prioritizing personal, marital, and family commitments in relation to professional commitments

- Engaging in regular exercise, hobbies, friendships, emotional enrichment, artistic endeavors, and spiritual pursuits

What Psychological Treatments are Available for Adults with PTSD?

There are many treatments for PTSD, all of which share similar general stages and focus of treatment issues. These are reviewed followed by the specific treatments that can generally be categorized as:

- Global Therapies

- Individual Therapies

- Family/Marriage Therapies

- Group Therapies

- Social Rehabilitative Therapies

General Stages and Focus of Treatment

There are a number of treatments for PTSD, some of which encourage the client to specifically remember and focus on the experienced trauma (trauma-focus treatment). Others encourage the client to increase coping skills for current here-and-now stresses to improve daily functioning and decrease PTSD

If we don't take good care of ourselves, we will not be able to help others.

A program in Boston, dedicated to treating victims of sexual abuse and domestic violence, provides time-limited group treatment for clinicians and human service professionals who, themselves, were previously exposed to sexual trauma.[48]

The most current, comprehensive, and authoritative source on PTSD treatment, research, and practice is Effective Treatments for PTSD.[49] Much of the following information has been drawn from that source.

symptoms. In general, however, most clinicians who work with PTSD clients agree that therapy can be divided into three different stages:[40, 50]

1. **Establishing trust and safety**

2. **Trauma focus vs. supportive treatment**

3. **Integration**

Establishing Trust and Safety

It is emotionally dangerous for PTSD clients to relinquish the cognitive, emotional, and behavioral avoidant strategies they use to cope with intolerable intrusive recollections and arousal symptoms. As a result, clinicians must establish an atmosphere of trust and safety, thereby "earning the right to gain access" to carefully guarded, traumatic material.[51 (p. 806)]

Trauma Focus vs. Supportive Therapy

Trauma focus therapy encourages clients to explore traumatic material in depth, gaining authority over traumatic memories and taking control of their lives. As described in subsequent sections, it can be conducted in individual or group contexts with techniques that vary from *psychodynamic approaches* to *cognitive behavioral approaches*.[52-53] However, trauma focus treatment is not beneficial for all clients.

psychodynamic approaches — *therapeutic approaches that focus on unconscious and conscious motivations and drives*

cognitive behavioral approaches — *therapeutic approaches that focus on how patterns of thinking are shaped by reinforcement, learning, and conditioning models*

Most research data on trauma focus treatments apply only to those clients who have agreed to undergo such treatment. Although scientific evidence shows that trauma focus treatments have proven to be the most effective treatments to date (see below), some clients have absolutely no wish to revisit traumatic material because:

• They want to put the past behind them.

• They fear that they cannot tolerate the intrusive and arousal symptoms exacerbated by such memories.

supportive PTSD treatments — *PTSD treatments that encourage skill building and problem solving for current issues in the client's life as an avenue for increasing adaptive functioning and regaining a sense of control*

Indeed, there is evidence that *supportive PTSD treatments* that deliberately avoid traumatic material to promote problem solving and adaptive coping in a here-and-now context may not only be beneficial but may actually be the treatment of choice for some with PTSD. Researchers need to develop better guidelines for pinpointing (in advance) which clients are the best candidates for trauma focus therapy.

There are a number of trauma focus and supportive PTSD treatments from which to choose, many of which are used in combination.[49]

Integration

Having obtained such authority and control, clients are now ready to disconnect from their preoccupation with traumatic memories and to reconnect with family, friends, and society. Indeed, when clients reach this stage, they really don't want to devote valuable therapy time to traumatic material. Instead, they want to concentrate on current issues concerning marriage, family, work, etc.[40, 50-51]

Global Therapies

Global Therapies that are helpful with most trauma survivors and can be used in combination with individual and group therapies, include:

- **Psychological Debriefing** – Interventions used shortly after exposure to a catastrophe.

- **Psychoeducational Approaches** – Clients learn about common symptoms and experiences suffered by those with PTSD and ASD.

- **Peer Counseling** – Victims of trauma help each other, typically in group settings.

Psychological Debriefing

Many people believe that the best approach for those who experience a catastrophic event is early detection and timely intervention, referred to as Psychological Debriefing. Proponents of Psychological Debriefing assert that it can abort the onset of a serious mental disorder, can reduce severity and duration once it has taken hold, or can prevent Acute Stress Disorder (ASD) from progressing to a chronic and incapacitating state.

The best known form of Psychological Debriefing, Critical Incident Stress Debriefing (CISD), has been significantly modified from its original format by a number of trauma experts; therefore, this discussion uses the more general term, Psychological Debriefing.

In 1983, Jeffrey Mitchell developed a technique that he called, "Critical Incident Stress Debriefing (CISD)," which has formed the basis for the variety of psychological debriefing approaches currently utilized by disaster workers worldwide.[56]

Psychological Debriefing began in military psychiatry.[54-55] Researchers found that active duty personnel who had an incapacitating anxiety attack (e.g., "battle fatigue" or "combat stress reaction") responded better if treated at a medical unit close to the war zone [such as a mobile army surgical hospital, (MASH) unit]. The three main components of military Psychological Debriefing, Proximity, Immediacy, and Expectancy (PIE), were thought to produce rapid resolution of battle fatigue and prevent the later development of what is now called PTSD.

- **Proximity** means providing intervention at a location as close to the active combat zone as possible.

- **Immediacy** means intervening as soon as possible after the onset of battle fatigue.

- **Expectancy** means providing education that the acute stress reaction is a normal human response to an overwhelming and abnormal event. Included here is the expectation that the individual will quickly recover and return to military duties within a few days without immediate or long-term consequences from the acute stress reaction.

The success of the PIE approach in the military setting fostered the use of similar interventions for those who experienced natural disasters like an earthquake, hurricane, or flood, or man-made catastrophes such as a large-scale terrorist bombing or an airplane crash.

The seven general components of Psychological Debriefing, often conducted in groups of 10-20, include:[57-58]

1. **The Introduction:** The debriefer (group leader) introduces him/herself, establishes his/her own credibility, and explains that the group will emphasize confidentiality so that people feel free to participate fully in the process without fear of subsequent consequences for being truthful.

2. **Expectations and Facts:** The debriefer encourages participants to factually report what they witnessed and what they expected during the traumatic event from their unique vantage points.

3. **Thoughts and Impressions:** Participants review their thoughts and sensory impressions (e.g., sights, sounds, smells, etc.) during the traumatic event.

4. **Emotional Reactions:** The debriefer encourages group members to share painful and previously unexpressed

emotional reactions to the catastrophe that might have killed a loved one, destroyed their homes, or injured them severely. This is when people have the opportunity to express feelings of fear, helplessness or horror (e.g., the ASD/PTSD A_2 criterion) or to express other overwhelming emotions such as grief, rage, or guilt.

5. **Normalization:** The sharing of such intense personal information gives group members a chance to ventilate powerful feelings and learn that others have had similar reactions. This enables them to realize that their emotions are similar to others and are normal.

6. **Future Planning/Coping:** The debriefer next informs the group that it is quite natural for some people to have disturbing symptoms shortly after a traumatic event such as insomnia, traumatic nightmares, avoidant symptoms, emotional numbing, jumpiness (e.g., startle responses), hypervigilence, and dissociative symptoms. Group members are encouraged to speak about such symptoms they have experienced. The focus here is on how best to deal with such symptoms through internal coping mechanisms and external (social) support.

7. **Disengagement:** The debriefer may distribute psychoeducational materials that describe the normal human response to catastrophic stress to foster for most, if not all group members, the understanding that the intense emotional reaction and psychological symptoms currently reported by group members can be expected to subside within weeks. Group members are cautioned, however, that if this is not the case for them and if intense emotional reactions or psychological symptoms are presently intolerable or if they persist beyond a month that they should consider seeking professional assistance for their distress. The debriefer will offer to provide a list of mental health professionals to those interested after the group session ends.

How Effective is Psychological Debriefing?

Little evidence exists that Psychological Debriefing cures ASD or prevents PTSD. Most studies find that trauma survivors who received Psychological Debriefing did not experience a lower incidence of PTSD in comparison to those who did not receive debriefing. Indeed, some well-designed studies have found worsening, rather than improvement of PTSD symptoms among debriefing recipients. On the other hand, these same studies show that 50-90 percent of debriefing recipients believe that this intervention facilitated their recovery from the emotional impact of the traumatic event.[58]

Psychoeducation

The first step in any therapeutic undertaking is to make sure that clients understand the nature of PTSD and its effect on them. It is relatively easy to move from a comprehensive diagnostic assessment (see chapter 2) into this phase by showing clients how their various reexperiencing, avoidant/numbing, and arousal symptoms fit into a coherent syndrome. Clients need to understand that they are not losing their minds (as many of them genuinely fear to be the case); that their constellation of symptoms has a specific name; and that many other people have suffered in a similar way after exposure to catastrophic stress. The advantages of psychoeducational intervention make it a very powerful and productive way to initiate any therapeutic activity. Specific benefits include Normalization, Removing Self-Blame & Self-Doubt, Correcting Misnderstandings, and Clinician Credibility.

Education about PTSD engenders hope that if their problem "has a name," there must be known treatment interventions.

Normalization — Just telling people that the nature of their post-traumatic emotional disturbance is no different than the experience of millions of men, women, and children exposed to similar stresses engenders a profound sense of relief in most people.

Such information helps them recognize that they're not losing their minds, that there's no stigma attached to this kind of all-too-human response to an overwhelming experience, and that they don't have to be ashamed of having PTSD symptoms.

There are always heroes and heroines who rise to extraordinary challenges with incredible courage, cunning, and success (as in the myths and legends of every culture since the beginnings of oral history) but most of us are not glorified by how we may have behaved during a catastrophe.

Removing Self-Blame & Self-Doubt — Telling clients that PTSD is fundamentally about being in the wrong place at the wrong time, and being overwhelmed by a stressor with which no one could have been expected to cope, is a powerful message that most clients can hear readily. It is an important message to deliver very quickly because most humans do not face these overwhelming events as they would have wished. Therefore, psychoeducation on the normal human response to overwhelming stress and (more importantly) on the normal human emotional response during the aftermath of a traumatic event helps survivors:

- Set their actions and reactions into an appropriate context
- Understand their PTSD symptoms in this context (relieving them of self-blame)
- Understand that they are not losing their minds
- Become motivated for treatment

Correcting Misunderstandings — Another important benefit of psychoeducation is that the PTSD model helps people understand disturbing behavior that has been interpreted erroneously. For example, a wife who blames herself for the sexual and emotional withdrawal of her spouse will learn that this is not a personal rejection but rather the expression of her husband's PTSD avoidant/numbing symptoms due to a traumatic event; reframing the problem can focus treatment and often save a marriage before things deteriorate beyond repair.

Clinician Credibility — The final advantage of psychoeducation is that it quickly lets clients know that the clinician understands their problem at its most fundamental level. It is a rapid and effective communication that the clinician deserves trust and is qualified to treat them, helping them make sense of their disturbing and disruptive symptoms.

How Effective is Psychoeducational Therapy for PTSD?

There has been no systematic evaluation of psychoeducation as a stand-alone PTSD treatment. However, there is a strong consensus among clinicians that it is a very important component of any therapeutic approach.

Peer Counseling

Peer Counseling, a powerful group process for PTSD sufferers is similar to Alcoholics Anonymous, with unique attributes including:

1. Everyone who participates has done so because they want to take control of their lives by seeking more effective ways to cope with their PTSD symptoms.

2. There is no authority figure such as a doctoral-level clinician. Instead everyone is an equal authority based on his or her own personal experience. Participants are simultaneously clients and clinicians, able to give and receive assistance to one another through honest disclosure and

An impressive example of psychoeducation occurred after the Loma Prieta Earthquake in California in 1989. Immediately afterward, pamphlets written in English and Spanish were distributed that described the normal reactions to traumatic stress (e.g., nightmares, startle responses, avoidant symptoms, irritability) and encouraged people to seek help if such symptoms were either too disturbing or too persistent. There were even coloring books with English and Spanish captions for young children so that they could express the emotional impact that the earthquake had had on them.

Vet Centers for war-zone veterans deliberately establish Peer Counseling groups away from hospitals and in neighborhood settings to underscore the egalitarian, community-based readjustment exemplified by this approach.

Peer Counseling can be found in high schools where adolescents, coping with physical and sexual abuse at home, consult peers who have faced the same challenges. They receive empathy and support from peers whom they can trust to respect absolute confidentiality. This often encourages them to seek more substantive help from adult professionals.

genuine response in the context of absolute trust and confidentiality.

An example of Peer Counseling can be found in rape crisis centers and battered women's shelters. Here the counselors have survived their own sexual trauma and/or domestic violence, found meaning in their suffering, and transformed their personal suffering into knowledge that they use to help others cope with similar experiences. It is reaffirming to women who seek such assistance to know that others before them have been able to pick up the pieces of their shattered lives and move on to a future that is gratifying and productive.

How Effective is Peer Counseling?

Since Peer Counseling is a consumer-driven approach that excludes professional clinicians, it does not lend itself to scientific research protocols in which some clients receive active treatment while others do not. It is clear that people who continue to participate in Peer Counseling do so because they find it beneficial.

Individual Psychotherapies

Clinicians primarily use three different types of individual psychotherapy to treat PTSD. These therapies can be used in combination with any of the other therapies and focus on PTSD symptoms through various methods. The primary therapies include:

- Cognitive Behavioral Therapy (CBT)
- Psychodynamic Psychotherapy
- Eye Movement Desensitization Reprocessing (EMDR)

Cognitive Behavioral Therapy (CBT)

Cognitive Behavioral Therapy is based on principles of learning and conditioning. Given the fact that PTSD develops when exposure to an overwhelming stimulus (the Criterion A_1 event) elicits a profound emotional reaction (the Criterion A_2 response) it is understandable why learning and conditioning models have provided such a powerful conceptual approach to PTSD. The sudden, intense, anxiety experienced by Mary T. in response to the sight or sound of a large tractor-trailer truck is an excellent example of fear conditioning. Here the traumatic stimulus (the truck) automatically evokes the post-traumatic emotional response (fear, helplessness and horror). The intensity of this emotional reaction provokes avoidant behaviors that will reduce the emotional impact of such a stimulus. Successful reduction of fear/helplessness/horror will, in turn, reinforce such avoidant behavior so that it will be repeated in the future in response to traumatic stimuli.

Many PTSD symptoms can be formulated in terms of standard psychological conditioning, which occurs in a two-stage process:

1. The fear conditioning in which a trauma-related stimulus automatically evokes intrusion and hyperarousal symptoms

2. The avoidant behavior activated by the powerful and intolerable psychological response in the first stage

Successful reduction of intrusion/hyperarousal symptoms will increase the likelihood that avoidant behaviors will be repeated in the future because of their protective value.

Various CBT approaches are designed to counteract these conditioned responses by attacking this two-stage process with different techniques. The ultimate goal is to normalize the abnormal feelings, thoughts, and behaviors exhibited by individuals with PTSD. CBT has proven to be the best treatment for PTSD in the current published literature.

Cognitive Behavioral techniques used in PTSD treatment are most often used in combination with each other and include:[53, 59-60]

- **Exposure Therapy** – Techniques aimed at disconnecting the overwhelming sense of fear from trauma memories

- **Cognitive Therapy** – Techniques focused on relearning thoughts and beliefs generated from the traumatic event, which impede current coping skills

- **Cognitive Processing Therapy (CPT)** – Techniques that focus on both the emotional and the cognitive consequences of trauma exposure

- **Stress Inoculation Training (SIT)** – A variety of anxiety management techniques designed to increase coping skills for current situations

- **Systematic Desensitization** – A technique designed to help clients substitute a relaxation response for the anxiety response typically elicited by a reminder of the trauma

- **Assertiveness Training** – A technique focusing on replacing an assertive response for the anxiety response typically elicited by a trauma reminder

- **Biofeedback and Relaxation Training** – Anxiety management techniques used to help clients master overwhelming anxiety feelings elicited by a trauma reminder

Exposure Therapy

Developed to separate the traumatic memory from the conditioned emotional response so that it no longer has the power to dominate thoughts, feelings, and behavior, Exposure Therapy uses Imaginal Exposure, exposure to traumatic stimuli through mental imagery. [53, 59-62] Additionally, In-Vivo Exposure, in which clients confront the actual scene of the traumatic event, is also used in Exposure Therapy.

Clinicians ask clients receiving Imaginal Exposure to narrate the traumatic event. If there have been a number of traumatic episodes (as with survivors of recurrent child abuse, domestic violence, war trauma, or torture), the clinicians asks clients to construct narratives about the worst events they clearly remember. The clinician prompts clients to close their eyes and visualize (imagine) what happened while repeating the narrative several times during a single session. Initially, clients will experience great anxiety as they begin to imagine themselves back in the traumatic situation. They are asked to rate the level of subjective distress every 10 minutes on a 10-100 *Subjective Units of Distress Scale (SUDS)*, where 10 is no distress and 100 is the most fear/helplessness/horror they have ever experienced. Distress levels are usually in the 70-90 range during initial Imaginal Exposure sessions. However, through repeated exposure to the traumatic memory, clients experience a progressive reduction in distress levels so that they may fall to the 10-20 range by the end of a single session and remain at negligible levels by the end of an 8- to 10-session Exposure Therapy treatment.

Subjective Units of Distress Scale — a scale ranging from 10-100 with 10 being the least anxiety provoking and 100 being the most anxiety provoking. The SUDS scoring system allows the client to express exactly how upsetting or distressing certain stimuli are in comparison to other anxiety experiences

Exposure Therapy abolishes the first-stage, conditioned emotional response evoked by traumatic stimuli. Clients recognize that the traumatic memories are just memories and cannot harm them in any way. Following successful exposure treatment, clients can confront these memories without having the recollections trigger intrusive/hyperarousal PTSD symptoms. If the conditioned emotional response can be abolished, avoidant symptoms are no longer relevant. This is

Successful Exposure Therapy nips the sequence of PTSD symptoms in the bud.

undoubtedly why this approach has proven to be the most effective treatment for PTSD so far.

Cognitive Therapy

Cognitive Therapy addresses the thoughts and beliefs generated by the traumatic event rather than the conditioned emotional response addressed by Exposure Therapy.[63-67] Cognitive Therapy focuses on how individuals with PTSD have interpreted the traumatic event with respect to their appraisals about the world and themselves. For example, those who have been overwhelmed by a catastrophic stressor typically perceive the world as dangerous and themselves as incompetent. As a result, PTSD clients see themselves as perennial victims powerless to cope with life and take charge of their personal destiny. Such a belief system then becomes a hard-wired, self-fulfilling prophecy.

> **Example**
>
> Mary T.'s persistent inability to overcome her PTSD symptoms and resume her life as before has destroyed her confidence in herself. She has come to think of herself as a failure, someone unable to cope with even minor stressors. Because of this pervasive sense of personal inadequacy, she is easily overwhelmed and unable to perform routine tasks. It is a vicious circle since the more she fails to perform, the more she feels inadequate, and the more she finds the world overwhelming.

In Cognitive Therapy, the first step is to identify automatic thoughts (such as Mary's thoughts about herself) and to understand that although originally developed from the trauma, these thoughts currently hinder adaptive functioning. Second, the therapy focuses on correcting erroneous thoughts with more accurate information, replacing automatic, dysfunctional thoughts with more realistic and adaptive ones. Successful cognitive therapy creates an accurate appraisal of:

- Situations as either safe or dangerous rather than believing automatically that all external events are dangerous.

> **Example**
>
> Mary T. needs to learn that there is nothing inherently dangerous about trucks or about driving a car. She needs to separate the specific tragic circumstances of her personal trauma from the trauma-related generalizations that currently make her afraid to travel on the highway.

- One's own strengths and weaknesses in different situations rather than an automatic belief that one is personally incompetent and unable to cope with life's challenges.

> **Example**
>
> Mary T. needs to understand that what happened during the accident was not due to a failure on her part. She also needs to learn that her current immobility is due to PTSD and not due to her own personal inadequacies.

Clinicians often combine Cognitive Therapy with Exposure Therapy to work on both the conditioned emotional response and inaccurate appraisals about the world and oneself. One somewhat different approach for combining Cognitive and Exposure Therapy is Cognitive Processing Therapy (CPT).

Cognitive Processing Therapy (CPT)

CPT addresses both the emotional and cognitive consequences of trauma exposure to alter erroneous beliefs about oneself and the world so that clients can access and process the natural emotions that have been distorted and obscured by their personal interpretations of the traumatic event.[68-70] Clinicians ask participants to write a thorough account of their traumatic experiences. CPT is similar to Exposure Therapy except the narratives are written by clients rather than elicited by the therapist. The written format gives the CPT client more control over the pace and intensity of disclosure than is the case in exposure treatment.

According to CPT theory, negative belief systems a person generates following a trauma (e.g., "I am powerless," "I am inadequate," "The world is a dangerous place,") make it impossible to process the normal emotional reactions produced by the catastrophic event (e.g., sadness and fear). This happens because the trauma survivor is preoccupied with inappropriate and intolerable emotions (e.g., guilt and shame) that evolve because of erroneous beliefs and interpretations about the traumatic experience. Only by confronting the distorted traumatic memories can clients challenge/modify these erroneous beliefs, thereby dissipating inappropriate emotions.

CPT is a technique that enables trauma survivors to move beyond distorted cognitions that affect normal and healthy processing of traumatic memories.

> **Example**
>
> Mary T.'s inappropriate feelings of guilt about the accident and shame about her current feelings of inadequacy have dominated her feelings about the traumatic event. They have prevented her from normal grieving about the loss of her husband, her marriage, her future, and the person she was before the accident. Psychological recovery depends upon moving beyond trauma-engendered cognitive distortions and inappropriate emotions so that she can freely process normal emotions (e.g., sadness and fear) that have been inaccessible up to this point.

Biofeedback and Relaxation Training

Biofeedback and Relaxation Training are ineffective stand-alone treatments but function as anxiety management techniques used with other CBT approaches, such as Stress Inoculation Training (SIT) (reviewed on page 51) and Systematic Desensitization (reviewed below).[59] Relaxation Training teaches clients to relax their musculature through breathing and meditation-like tensing and untensing exercises, often assisted by audio tapes. Learning to induce muscle relaxation helps control anxiety. Biofeedback is a process used to reduce tension and anxiety in which the clients learn information about their own physiological processes. For example, the client receives continuous feedback about heart rate, or muscle tension, learning to consciously control these processes. Treatment success is measured by volitional reductions in heart rate, muscle tension or other physiological processes.

Systematic Desensitization (SD)

This technique teaches clients to substitute a relaxation response for an anxiety response.[71] As adapted for PTSD, clinicians help clients recondition anxiety-provoking stimuli (e.g., trauma-related cues, which normally elicit an anxiety response) to be followed by a relaxation response.

In SD, the client is exposed to trauma-related stimuli (usually through imaginal exposure) with repeated interruptions during which relaxation techniques are practiced until the client responds to a previously anxiety-provoking stimulus with a relaxation response. *Habituation* is the foundation of this process through repeated presentation of trauma-related cues paired with relaxation. Generally, clinicians introduce trauma-related stimuli in order of increasing distress so that the clients may acquire progressive mastery (i.e., anxiety reduction) by starting with the least distressing and working gradually up to the most distressing stimulus. This is accomplished through having the client complete a Subjective Units of Distress Scale (SUDS) in which they list anxiety provoking stimuli and rank order from least distressing to most distressing.

habituation — gradual, naturally occurring reduction of anxiety or discomfort over time, if exposure is maintained

SD differs from Exposure Therapy in two important ways:

1. Exposure to trauma-related stimuli is much longer and more intense with Exposure Therapy.

2. In Exposure Therapy, clients begin their work with their most distressing traumatic material first rather than starting with least distressing material as in SD. Both approaches, however, utilize the SUDS scoring system to monitor subjective distress throughout the therapy session.

Assertiveness Training

Assertiveness Training is based on the same reciprocal inhibition principle employed in Systematic Desensitization except that the incompatible response is an assertive (rather than a relaxation) response.

Not useful as stand-alone PTSD treatment, Assertiveness Training is a distinct component within other CBT approaches mentioned, such as Stress Inoculation Training (SIT) (reviewed on page 51) and Cognitive Processing Therapy (CPT) (reviewed on pages 48-49).[72] Assertiveness Training teaches a client to become more self-assertive and self-confident in interpersonal relationships. It teaches clients to report their feelings and beliefs (both positive and negative) directly and honestly. Such training is often conducted through role playing in the therapeutic setting and practiced in actual situations. Proponents believe that assertive behavior is incompatible with anxiety. For Mary T., this treatment would promote immediate disclosure of her emotional state to prevent anxiety-driven, avoidant behavior.[73-74]

Stress Inoculation Training (SIT)

Originally adapted for treating rape victims, SIT provides PTSD clients with a repertoire of tools and skills that they can utilize to control anxiety elicited either by trauma-related stimuli or during threatening situations.[73-74] It combines relaxation training, biofeedback training, and Assertiveness Training and utilizes:

- **Social skills training**[59] — clinicians help clients increase specific interpersonal skills necessary for positive relationships.

- **Role playing**[59] — clinicians practice with clients how they can respond in specific situations.

- **Distraction techniques**[59] — clinicians teach clients to yell "stop" to themselves each time certain thoughts start.

How Effective are Cognitive Behavioral Techniques?

Cognitive Behavioral Therapy is the most proven treatment for PTSD to date, although differences exist among different CBT approaches (as shown below). CBT treatments are generally carefully scripted in treatment manuals and usually require 9-16 sessions.

The following results of CBT efficacy studies to date are excerpted from an excellent recent comprehensive review on CBT for the treatment of PTSD:[59]

- **Exposure Therapy**[59] — PTSD symptoms were reduced by 26-80 percent across 13 different studies with the preponderance of results indicating improvement greater than 60 percent in all three PTSD symptom clusters. Improvements were maintained at six months (two studies) and 12 months (one study).

- **Cognitive Therapy**[59] — Two studies comparing Cognitive Therapy with Exposure Therapy found both equally effective, producing 60-70 percent improvement in PTSD symptoms.

- **Exposure plus Cognitive Therapy**[59] — Given the efficacy of each treatment separately, one might expect that combining these two CBT treatments would produce better results. This has not been the case. Combined Exposure/Cognitive treatment results in the same success rate as either treatment alone, producing the same 60-70

SIT reduces avoidance behavior through anxiety reduction and fosters a sense of personal competence.

There are more published, well-controlled studies on CBT than on any other PTSD treatment. Furthermore, treatment effects appear greater with CBT than with any other treatment.

For those individuals diagnosed with Acute Stress Disorder, a recent study found that prolonged (i.e., 50 minutes) Exposure Therapy successfully prevented the development of PTSD in 80 percent of the participants.[75]

Exposure Therapy with or without Cognitive Therapy has been tested with survivors of a greater variety of traumatic events than other treatments. These include clients traumatized by sexual assault, war-zone exposure, or childhood sexual abuse.

percent symptom reduction obtained with the other treatment alone.

- **Cognitive Processing Therapy (CPT)** — There are three CPT studies conducted with clients having rape-related PTSD. In one study, CPT performed as well as Exposure Therapy; while in another, all clients had significant reduction in all three PTSD symptom clusters, and none continued to meet PTSD diagnostic criteria at the six-month follow-up.[68, 70]

- **Stress Inoculation Training (SIT)** — Four studies on women with rape-related PTSD have tested SIT alone or in combination with Exposure Therapy. In all cases, results from SIT were equal to those from Exposure Therapy, producing a 60-70 percent reduction in PTSD symptom severity. Three-month follow-up assessments showed substantial improvement in one study and improvement slightly better with Exposure Therapy than SIT in another study.[59, 73-74]

- **Systematic Desensitization** — This approach has been tested in six studies, mostly with Vietnam combat veterans, but also with clients who had been exposed to rape and interpersonal violence. Almost all of these results were published before 1990 because most CBT clinicians now favor the longer exposures of Exposure Therapy over the shorter exposures of Systematic Desensitization. Furthermore, Exposure Therapy has proven a much more effective PTSD treatment than Systematic Desensitization.[59]

Exposure Therapy, Cognitive Therapy, and the combination, significantly outperformed Relaxation Therapy in treatment.

- **Biofeedback and Relaxation Therapy** — These have performed poorly as stand-alone PTSD treatments. In three studies, clients receiving one or both of these approaches demonstrated no greater improvement than comparison groups receiving no treatment. However, clinicians see both treatments as useful and complementary components in combination with other CBT therapies. This combination makes it impossible to delineate the unique contribution that these therapies have made to the overall CBT treatment package.[59]

- **Assertiveness Training** — This method has been tested once with clients with rape-related PTSD. Although slightly less effective than SIT, producing 40-60 percent reduction in PTSD symptoms, this difference is not statistically significant. Further research is needed to assess the efficacy of Assertiveness Training as a stand-alone-treatment although it is often included as a component of SIT and CBT.[59, 74]

Psychodynamic Psychotherapy

Psychodynamic psychotherapy has been used to treat post-traumatic disorders for over 100 years. Psychodynamic theory focuses on *psychic balance*, which sometimes can only be achieved when the client forces intolerable thoughts and feelings out of conscious awareness through the process called *repression*. However, these now unconscious traumatic memories are still powerful enough to become expressed as symptoms, such as PTSD's intrusion, avoidant/numbing, and hyperarousal symptoms.[76]

Psychodynamic treatment seeks to understand the context of the traumatic memories and the defensive processes through which the unconscious transforms repressed memories into the maladaptive symptoms that initially drive treatment. Psychodynamic clinicians presume that those exhibiting PTSD symptoms have an abnormal psychological balance due to repressed memories and symptom formation. According to psychoanalytic theory, simply focusing on symptom reduction can achieve little as long as repressed memories remain.[76]

Using a process called "working through," the clinician helps the client understand the meaning of each unconscious process to achieve a balance between traumatic memories, external demands, and subjective needs. "Working through" requires the clinician to maintain a stance of *neutrality* within the intense, therapeutic relationship. This allows clients to *project* feelings about significant others onto the clinician, bringing feelings and behaviors related to major relationships in the client's life into the dynamic relationship between the client and clinician for thorough exploration. By exploring these feelings and behaviors, clients gain insight on how their repressed memories (along with associated thoughts and feelings) have been transformed into their current symptoms. Ideally, this awareness helps the client better control the repression defense and ultimately leads to fewer symptoms.[76]

Psychodynamic treatments vary from 12 sessions to seven or more years. Longer Psychodynamic treatments seek to create a fundamental change in psychic balance while briefer forms (12-15 sessions) seek to foster improved self-understanding and ego-strength.

Brief Psychodynamic Psychotherapy (BPP), conducted within 12-15 sessions, focuses on the traumatic event itself. Through the retelling of the trauma story to a calm, empathic,

psychic balance — a dynamic equilibrium state between those thoughts, feelings, memories, and urges the conscious mind can tolerate and those it cannot

repression — a hypothetical, unconscious process by which unacceptable (often trauma-related) thoughts and feelings are kept out of conscious awareness

Repression has a cost (i.e., symptoms), and this cost may be too high for normal functioning and psychic health.

neutrality — a psychoanalytic technique by which clinicians reveal as little of themselves as possible so that thoughts, memories, and feelings generated during therapy come from the client's intrapsychic processes rather than from an interpersonal relationship between client and clinician

project — the mechanism by which the client's intrapsychic processes infuse the therapeutic relationship

For more detailed information on PTSD Psychodynamic therapy, refer to resources by Herman, Horowitz, Krystal, and Lindy.[40, 76-79]

self-cohesion — *knowledge and integration of previously unconscious motivations*

BPP has similar goals as exposure/cognitive therapy although the conceptual underpinnings and therapeutic techniques are extremely different.

compassionate, and non-judgmental clinician, the client achieves a greater sense of *self-cohesion*, develops more adaptive defenses and coping strategies, and successfully modulates intense emotions that emerge during therapy.[79] While working through the traumatic memories, the clinician also addresses the linkage between post-traumatic distress and current life stress. Clients learn to identify current life situations and environmental triggers that set off traumatic memories and exacerbate PTSD symptoms.

How Effective is Psychodynamic Therapy?

Because Psychodynamic treatment focuses primarily on psychic processes rather than psychiatric symptoms, there exists only one randomized clinical trial on the efficacy of this treatment for reducing PTSD symptoms.

Voluminous and rich literature on psychoanalytic psychotherapy is, for the most part, derived from detailed case histories rather than from controlled clinical trials.[76, 81-83]

This study involved the use of BPP for 18 sessions and compared results with Hypnotherapy and Systematic Desensitization. BPP effectively reduced PTSD intrusion and avoidance symptoms by approximately 40 percent. This improvement was:[80]

- Sustained for three months

- Comparable to results from the other two treatments

- Significantly greater than a wait list group that received no treatment

Much more research is needed to demonstrate PTSD efficacy.

Eye Movement Desensitization and Reprocessing (EMDR)

saccadic eye movements — *quick eye movements, jumping from one point of fixation to another*

Proponents of EMDR believe that *saccadic eye movements* reprogram brain function so that the emotional impact of a trauma can be finally and completely resolved.[84-85] When conducting EMDR, the clinician instructs the client to imagine a painful, traumatic memory and an associated negative cognition (e.g., guilt, shame). Then, the client is asked to articulate an incompatible positive cognition (e.g., personal worth, self efficacy, trustworthiness). The clinician then has the client contemplate the traumatic memory while visually focusing on the rapid movement of the clinicians' fingers. After each set of 10-12 eye movements, the clinician asks the client to rate the strength of both the distressing memory and his/her belief in the positive cognition.

Despite the name of this therapy, research evidence suggests that eye movements don't appear necessary for EMDR to work.[86] In five out of six published studies comparing conventional EMDR to EMDR minus eye movements, clients who received EMDR minus eye movements did just as well as those who received conventional EMDR. Therefore, it is difficult to substantiate that eye movements form the crucial ingredient in EMDR and even more difficult to defend the hypothesis that EMDR reprograms the brain's processing of traumatic memories.

Because empirical evidence suggests that EMDR is effective in treating PTSD (despite the apparent unimportance of eye movements), more research is needed to understand the actual mechanism by which EMDR works. Some theorists believe that there are a number of important EMDR components that account for its appeal among clinicians as well as its therapeutic efficacy. Among these are:[87]

- EMDR explicitly supports a belief that therapy will lead to positive growth.

- Clients select the traumatic material, which they process in their own ways and at their own paces — in this regard, EMDR differs markedly from the very directive approach utilized in Exposure Therapy.

- The focus on replacing negative with positive cognition has the same salutary effects as in Cognitive Therapy.

- Accessing emotions through these cognitions has the same positive impact as in Cognitive Processing Therapy (CPT).

- EMDR bypasses the intense interpersonal issues between client and clinician that are especially emphasized in the transference reaction in psychoanalytic psychotherapy.

- The clinician has an action to perform (e.g., finger movements) in addition to the traditional clinician role of active listening.

How Effective is EMDR in Treating PTSD?

Several studies show that in comparison with wait list clients who show little improvement, approximately two-thirds of those receiving EMDR no longer met the PTSD diagnostic criteria (i.e., they had a significant reduction in intrusion, avoidance/numbing, and hyperarousal symptom clusters). Research also indicates EMDR is superior to Psychodynamic,

Because EMDR is derived from and contains many elements of Cognitive Behavioral Therapy, (e.g., Exposure, Cognitive Processing, and Systematic Desensitization), some clinicians conclude that EMDR is really a variant of CBT and should not be considered a unique therapeutic approach. EMDR adherents sharply disagree, insisting that any resemblance to CBT is superficial. They assert that EMDR is a fundamentally new and different therapeutic approach.

Relaxation, or Supportive Therapies. Published results indicate that following treatment, 50-77 percent of clients receiving EMDR no longer meet criteria for the PTSD diagnosis in comparison to 20-50 percent receiving supportive therapy or treatment as usual.[86]

It is important to emphasize that this is only one study. More research is clearly needed to determine the efficacy of EMDR relative to CBT.

In examining what is the best psychotherapeutic treatment for PTSD, current evidence suggests that CBT is best. One head-to-head comparison between the two has been done in which PTSD clients who were randomized either to CBT (exposure/cognitive therapy) or EMDR had significantly better results with CBT than with EMDR. At the three-month follow-up, 58 percent CBT compared with 18 percent EMDR clients had recovered from PTSD.[88]

Marital/Family Therapies

Family members often cannot understand why a partner, parent, or child who had been loving and spontaneous before a trauma has metamorphosed into a distant, fearful stranger who cannot tolerate closeness or strong emotional expression.

Used best in combination with the other therapies, Marital/Family Therapy focuses on symptom relief through increasing help and understanding in the family unit. Clinicians often use Marital and Family Therapy to treat PTSD because the client's symptoms can produce a major disruption for the entire family. Symptoms such as irritability, jumpiness (e.g., startle), and hypervigilance may be so extreme as to appear like paranoia and can engender fear, frustration, confusion, and a sense of powerlessness in family members because they are so intense, bizarre, and difficult to understand. Family members end up in a perpetual state of anxiety and hypervigilance, "walking on eggshells" and doing their best not to say or do anything that will trigger a PTSD-related outburst. They struggle with how to help this difficult and unpredictable person whom they love and cannot understand. The marriage or family suffers from *secondary traumatization.*[89]

secondary traumatization — *the feelings, personal distress, and symptoms that are sometimes evoked in people who live with an individual who has PTSD*

Additionally, avoidant/numbing symptoms prevent normal emotional expression and behavioral closeness. As a result, family members are forced to operate within a domestic context in which intimacy is impossible. Since family members don't understand that this loss of intimacy is a PTSD symptom, they blame themselves, sometimes becoming depressed and often withdrawing to protect themselves from additional disappointments. Marital or Family Therapy helps alleviate these problems and promotes a more salutary healing environment for the partner, parent, or child with PTSD.

Family Therapy involves one or both of the following:[90]

1. **Systemic treatment** — Disrupted relationships, resulting from one family member's PTSD, receive primary attention. Family members focus on interpersonal dynamics, communication skills, and emotional expression. Treatment success is measured in terms of family function, cohesion, and communication.

2. **Supportive treatment** — To promote a better healing environment for the PTSD client, this treatment uses education about PTSD and communication with the PTSD sufferer, helping family members provide necessary support. Treatment success is measured in terms of the client's PTSD symptom reduction.

Some excellent sources for additional information on PTSD-related Marital and Family Therapy include writings by Riggs, Figley, Johnson or Harris.[90-96]

How Effective is Marital and Family Therapy?

There have been no research studies done on the effectiveness of either systemic or supportive Marital/Family Therapy for PTSD treatment. However, clinical wisdom and the successful application of Marital/Family Therapy in other psychiatric disorders indicate that spouses and families be included in treatment for partners, parents, or children with PTSD.[90]

Group Therapies

Group therapies utilize either a psychodynamic focus, CBT focus, or supportive techniques and can be used in combination with the other therapies. In all cases, trauma survivors learn about PTSD and help each other with the aid of a professional clinician.

Group therapy is effective and popular for those who have all survived the same type of trauma (e.g., war, rape, torture, terrorist bombing, etc.). As members share experiences, they become connected to one another by recognizing their common human fears, frailties, guilt, shame, and demoralization. Through clinician guidance, validation and normalization of these thoughts, feelings, and behaviors progresses to acquisition of more adaptive coping strategies, symptom reduction, and/or derivation of meaning from the traumatic experience. There are three different types of therapy groups, each with a different focus:[97]

Psychodynamic Focus Group Therapy

During the retelling of the trauma story, emotion is mobilized and hopefully the client experiences a profound catharsis or "abreaction." Achieving catharsis is an important mediator of recovery in this treatment approach.

Group members help one another understand how their assumptions about themselves (e.g., weak, shameful, guilty, undeserving) have been shaped and distorted by their traumatic experiences. By revisiting this material in the safety of the group, they are empowered to confront the traumatic memories to gain new insight about these memories and themselves, and integrate such knowledge into their lives. Personal growth results from improved ego strength and self-understanding. While symptom reduction is not the major treatment goal, theorists expect resolution of trauma-related disruptions to normal psychic processes will promote PTSD amelioration.[97-98]

Cognitive Behavioral Focus Group Therapy

The ultimate goal for both Psychodynamic and Cognitive Behavioral group therapy is for group members to gain "authority" over traumatic material so that it no longer becomes a dominant factor in their lives.[40]

These groups embody the concepts and approaches described earlier for individual Cognitive Behavioral Therapy[69, 97] (see pages 44-52). One specific group approach uses Exposure and Cognitive Therapy, where the clinician guides one group member at a time through a typical exposure session followed by cognitive restructuring.[99] During the exposure session, the other members are vicariously exposed to their own traumatic memories through observing someone else's treatment.

Group members do more for each other than provide social support. They validate one another's post-traumatic reactions, share their struggles to cope with PTSD-related problems, and provide honest criticism of fellow members' maladaptive coping behavior based on accurate empathy and their own experiences. Since group time is limited, group members must carry out homework assignments in which they focus or expose themselves to traumatic material. This homework is done through writing exercises or by repeatedly listening to an audiotape previously recorded during a group session in which they underwent exposure to their own traumatic material.

Supportive Group Therapy

Supportive groups emphasize here-and-now issues and try to redirect discussion of past traumatic experiences to present problems or concerns.

Supportive Group Therapy focuses on members' current life issues.[97-98] The goal of treatment is not to revisit, reframe, or master traumatic material, but to discuss here-and-now issues. Traumatic consequences, as expressed by PTSD symptoms, are only relevant if they affect present-day functioning. To improve emotional and interpersonal comfort and overall functioning group members are encouraged to develop better interpersonal and coping skills, problem-solving skills, and more adaptive responses to predictable challenges.

How Effective are Group Treatments for PTSD?

There is a great deal of empirical support for Cognitive Behavioral focus group treatment. In three studies of CBT group treatments (including CPT, Assertiveness Training, and SIT) on women traumatized by childhood or adult sexual abuse, PTSD symptoms were reduced 30-60 percent with reductions in all PTSD symptom clusters measured. Improvement was sustained for six months in all studies. One CBT group treatment for combat veterans showed a 20 percent reduction in PTSD symptom severity.[68-70, 97-98]

There is very little empirical research with Psychodynamic focus group treatment for PTSD, and the few findings that have been reported are equivocal. In the one study of Psychodynamic group treatment with childhood sexual abuse survivors, PTSD symptom severity was reduced by 18 percent.[97]

Finally, one controlled trial of Supportive Group Therapy for female sexual assault survivors showed a 19-30 percent reduction in intrusion and avoidance symptoms that was maintained for six months.[68]

Social Rehabilitative Therapies

These therapies are used separately and sometimes in combination with Marriage/Family Therapy or Psychoeducation. With this approach, trauma victims gain necessary employment, housing, and other vital resources.

Some people with severe and chronic PTSD are so impaired that they are unable to sustain a marriage, support a family, maintain gainful employment, or even care for themselves. They may be homeless. They may live on the fringes of society, supported primarily through public sector programs. They may be found among clients with other persistent mental illnesses from whom they are superficially indistinguishable.[14] Such clients are not candidates for the individual, marital/family, and group psychotherapies described above. At this point in time, the recommended approach for these clients is psychosocial rehabilitation.

Psychoeducation is an important component of Supportive Group Therapy in which group members acquire information about the impact of PTSD symptoms on marital, familial, social, and vocational functioning.[100]

Other group approaches employing CBT have been utilized. Most notably, Cognitive Processing Therapy (CPT - see pages 48-49) originally developed for female sexual assault survivors.[68-70]

Stress Inoculation Training (page 51) and Assertiveness Training (page 50) have also been used as group therapies.[68, 70]

Psychosocial rehabilitation therapies offer a wide spectrum of interventions designed to improve the functional capacity, social interaction, and quality of life for those with PTSD who are the most severely avoidant and incapacitated.

There are seven psychosocial rehabilitation techniques recommended for clients with severe and chronic PTSD:[101]

1. **Client education services** — Information about the diagnosis and nature of PTSD, available treatments (e.g. medication), health needs, and high-risk behaviors (e.g. alcohol/substance abuse, HIV infection, etc.).

2. **Self-care/independent living skills techniques** — Interventions to promote personal care, personal hygiene, money management, shopping, cooking, using transportation, medication compliance, and recreation.

3. **Supported housing services** — Shelter for homeless individuals, assuring safety-adequacy/stability/affordability of current housing, or assistance making new living arrangements.

4. **Family support** — Interventions for both the client and family to reduce PTSD-induced alienation from the family and to involve the family in ongoing treatment.

5. **Social skills training** — Social-learning-based techniques designed to reduce PTSD-induced social isolation and promote satisfying interpersonal interactions.

6. **Supported employment techniques** — Placing a person with PTSD into a paid, productive activity of particular interest.

7. **Case management** — (Indicated for PTSD clients when they cannot locate and coordinate access to the psychosocial rehabilitative services described previously.) Ensures compliance with treatment plans for optimizing functional performance, avoiding relapse, and preventing rehospitalization.

How Effective are Social Rehabilitative Therapies?

Although psychosocial rehabilitation techniques have yet to be formally tested with PTSD clients, they have proven effective with chronic schizophrenia and other persistent mental impairments. Specifically, paid work activity has been associated with reduced symptomatology in people with schizophrenia.[102] Since these interventions appear to generalize well from clients with one mental disorder to another, it is reasonable to expect that they will also work with PTSD clients.

There is a great deal of empirically validated success with case management among those with severe mental disorders, many of whom probably had PTSD.[101]

This finding suggests that acquisition and mastery of skill in the social context of work may restore a sense of meaning and purpose to PTSD clients and may actually reduce symptom severity.[103-104]

What Psychological Treatments are Available for Children and Adolescents with PTSD, and How Effective Are Those Treatments?

Treatments for children and adolescents are often age-appropriate interventions extrapolated from adult treatment methods. For children who develop PTSD, the impact of the trauma as well as the expression of symptoms may be significantly affected by the developmental stage at which the trauma occurred.[105] For example:

- **Abused infants and toddlers** may have impaired ability to form attachments with significant others.

- **Traumatized pre-schoolers**, who lack the conceptual and communication capacities of older individuals, may express nonverbal symptoms (e.g., aggression, withdrawal, or sleep problems).

- **Trauma in children** may result in restructured emotional expression, social isolation, problems with impulse control, self-injurious behaviors, dissociation, and development of *Dissociative Identity Disorder* or *Borderline Personality Disorder*.

- **Trauma during adolescence** may severely disrupt normal adult development by producing problems in separation from parents, personality evolution, symbolic thinking, and moral development.[106-110]

A number of experts have written thoughtful articles on developmentally sensitive treatment approaches for children with PTSD.[111] There is a growing body of empirical evidence to guide us. Seven randomized research trials and other studies support using CBT for treatment of PTSD in children.[111] Additionally, clinicians use and consider helpful other treatment methods not yet tested in research studies, including play therapy, Stress Inoculation Training, and psychoeducation.

Cognitive Behavioral Therapy

One study using CBT in a group setting was conducted at school with 9- and 10-year-old survivors of Armenia's 1989 earthquake. This study reported 25-40 percent reductions in all three PTSD symptom clusters compared with a control group of children who received no treatment and showed worsening PTSD symptoms over the subsequent 18 months.[112] Another

Treatments for children and adolescents must take these factors into account, and be presented in a context and format that is developmentally sensitive.

Dissociative Identity Disorder – a mental disorder characterized by one's personality becoming so fragmented that pronounced changes in behavior and reactivity are noticed between different social situations or social roles.

Borderline Personality Disorder – a personality disorder characterized by extreme instabilities fluctuating between normal functioning and psychic disability.

research study addressed an 18-week, school-based group CBT treatment for children in grades 4-9 who had been exposed to a single-incident stressor (e.g., criminal assault, car accidents, natural disasters – in contrast to protracted physical or sexual abuse). Researchers reported significant reduction in all PTSD symptom clusters - by the end of treatment, 57 percent no longer met PTSD diagnostic criteria and 86 percent no longer had PTSD six months after treatment.[113] A third, school-based CBT approach successfully reduced depressive and anxiety symptoms among sexually abused preschool children, but PTSD symptoms were not monitored.[111] In summary, a consistent body of evidence supports the efficiency of CBT treatment for children with PTSD.

Psychological Debriefing

This approach proved effective following a sniper attack in a school[114] and in a well-controlled study of Hawaiian children who survived the massive destruction of Hurricane Iniki. Debriefing six months after the hurricane produced a 30-35 percent reduction in intrusion and avoidance symptoms among those children who received treatment.[115]

Art and Play Therapy

Because some (especially younger) children may find it difficult to participate in exposure treatment, researchers suggest that children may benefit more from indirect approaches such as *art therapy* and *play therapy*.[111]

art therapy – a treatment procedure in which clients express themselves through drawing, writing, dance, drama, or other creative media to access underlying emotions

play therapy – a technique for treating young children in which they reveal their problems on a fantasy level with dolls, clay, and other toys

Stress Inoculation Training (SIT)

Pairing SIT (see page 51) such as relaxation, thought stopping, and positive imagery with exposure treatment may result in reduced symptoms. This combination gives children tools to keep from being overwhelmed by the reactivated traumatic memories that emerge during exposure treatment. Some theorists argue that these tools also foster a sense of mastery and control that promotes recovery. SIT (plus gradual exposure) was rigorously tested in one randomized clinical trial with sexually abused children.[116]

Psychoeducational Approaches for Parents, Teachers and Children

It is important to include parents in treatments for children with PTSD. Many studies have shown that the parents' emotional reaction to the trauma and the amount of family support available to the child will have a significant impact on the child's symptoms.[111] The best predictor of a favorable outcome for children is if parents and other significant adults can cope with the trauma.[110] Therefore, Psychoeducation and Supportive Family Therapy described earlier (see pages 42-43 and 56-57) are especially relevant to PTSD treatment for children.[111]

There has been very little research on treatment for children with PTSD. However, the strongest findings, to date, indicate that the best results are achieved when the family is included in treatment, and that school-based CBT treatments may offer the most efficient and effective approach for many children.[111-113]

**Therapy Notes
from the Desk
of Pat Owen**

July 2

We've now completed five sessions of exposure coupled with cognitive therapy. We've had to go slow because traumatic material really provokes intense emotional arousal and even some mild dissociative symptoms. But we're making progress. Today, she was able to reduce her SUDS rating from 85 at the beginning to 40 by the end of the session. We've got five more sessions scheduled, and I'll add more, if necessary.

Besides progress in therapy, she's starting to function more effectively at home. Driving the car for short trips. Feels more like taking responsibility for housework. Even starting to spend some time at the computer. It may be time to start considering when she might be able to gradually return to work.

Chapter Four: Medical Treatments for PTSD

Diary of Mary T.

August 25

I've been on the drug for three weeks now. I really didn't want to take it, but Dr. Owen convinced me that it might help me function better. It's really getting easier to get behind the wheel of the car. I still don't like the trucks, but at least I can deal with them now. Therapy is really helpful. I can handle the memories a lot better and have begun to discover things that happened after the crash that I had completely forgotten. It's also easier to concentrate, and I can sit at the computer for a few hours. Dr. Owen wants me to consider easing back to work on a part-time basis. I don't think I'm ready, but I'll give it a try if she thinks I should.

This chapter answers the following:

- **How Does the Human Stress Response Relate to PTSD?** — This section covers the two major components of the human stress response: the Fight-or-Flight Reaction and the General Adaptation Syndrome.

- **What Psychobiological Abnormalities Exist for Those With PTSD?** — This section reviews the elements of abnormal functioning in human biological systems related to PTSD.

- **What Medical Treatments Are Used for PTSD?** — This section reviews the pharmacological treatments available and their efficacy for treating PTSD.

Medical treatments for PTSD target abnormalities in the multiple biological systems involved with a person's response to stress. This section reviews:

- The body's basic response to stress

- Abnormalities in this stress response for those suffering PTSD

- Specific medications that target these abnormalities along with corresponding research on treatment efficacy

How Does the Human Stress Response Relate to PTSD?

Through evolution, humans have acquired biological mechanisms for coping with the variety of stresses normally encountered in a lifetime. The two major components of the human

Note: Because clinical/medical settings most prominently use the word "patient" instead of "client," "patient" will be used in this chapter.

stress response are the Fight-or-Flight Reaction and the General Adaptation Syndrome.

Fight or Flight Reaction

sympathetic nervous system — *part of the autonomic nervous system that regulates arousal functions such as heart rate and blood flow*

This reaction refers to the mobilization of brain and *sympathetic nervous system (SNS)* mechanisms in response to a threat.[117] During this reaction, the heart pumps more blood to the muscles, which enables them to perform defensive ("fight") or escape ("flight") movements necessary for survival. The fight-or-flight reaction begins in the brain via a complex array of highly evolved neurobiological mechanisms that detect danger, experience fear, and set off the sequence of adaptive escape and defensive responses.

adrenergic response — *neuronal activation mediated by either noradrenaline or adrenaline*

Several important chemicals in the brain (neurotransmitters) and the SNS that relay signals from one neuron to the next mediate the fight-or-flight response. This "mediation" is known as the *adrenergic response* because these neurotransmitters are primarily noradrenaline and adrenaline (also known as norepinephrine and epinephrine). The many medications in current medical use that augment or attenuate the adrenergic response in the brain, heart, blood vessels, and elsewhere are called adrenergic agents.

See pages 70-71 for an explanation of how neurotransmitters function.

Only recently have clinicians really understood how the brain responds to threat in order to initiate the fight-or- flight response. When faced with a dangerous or stressful situation, the brain releases a hormone called "corticotropin releasing factor (CRF)," which activates the neurons in the locus coeruleus, a small cluster of nerve cells that contain most of the brain's adrenergic neurons. Locus coeruleus neurons stimulate brain centers that mediate arousal, emotional reactivity, and memory (e.g., the hypothalamus, amygdala, hippocampus and cerebral cortex) as well as the SNS, which instigates the fight-or-flight response. CRF activates an additional response to stress called "The General Adaptation Syndrome."

hypothalamic-pituitary-adrenocortical (HPA) axis — *refers to three anatomic structures that participate collectively in the hormonal response to stress: the hypothalamus (in the brain), the pituitary gland, and the outer layer (cortex) of the adrenal gland*

The General Adaptation Syndrome

The second major system that responds to stress is a hormonal rather than a neurotransmitter response and focuses on the *hypothalamic-pituitary-adrenocortical (HPA) axis.*[118] The hypothalamus, a small midline nucleus on the underside of the brain, releases CRF into the bloodstream, which carries it rapidly to the nearby pituitary gland where it provokes the release of adrenocorticotropic hormone (ACTH). ACTH is then carried by the blood stream to the adrenal gland (perched atop the kidney), which releases *cortisol*. Cortisol has been called the "stress hormone" because blood cortisol levels are elevated during the normal human response to stress.

cortisol — a hormone that increases energy by raising blood glucose levels, decreases immune processes, and has other metabolic and neurobiological actions

Serotonin is another neurotransmitter that is intimately involved in the functioning of both adrenergic and HPA mechanisms. Primarily located in the brainstem raphe nuclei, which have abundant reciprocal interactions with both the adrenergic and HPA systems, serotonin can facilitate the human stress response.[119] An important class of medications that enhance serotonergic activity are called Selective Serotonin Reuptake Inhibitors (SSRIs), some of which have proven effective for treating PTSD. The diagram below depicts the major areas of the brain involved in the human stress response. The following section reviews the abnormalities in this response resulting from trauma.

CRF is really the ignition switch for the human stress response since it activates both SNS and HPA reactions simultaneously.

Many other neurobiological systems participate in the human stress response including the immunological system, thyroid system, and other neurotransmitter and hormonal systems.[120]

Figure 4.1 — Human Stress Response

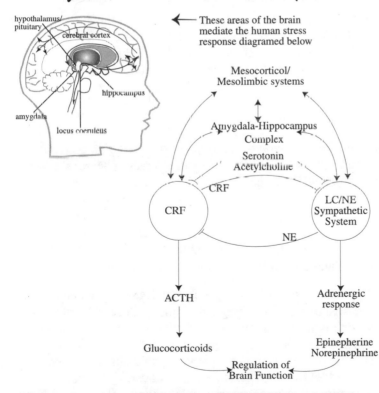

CRH-Corticotropin-Releasing Factor hormone; NE-norephinephrine; LC/NE-Locus Coruleus-Norepinephrine; ACTH-Corticotropin. Diagram adapted from and reprinted with permission of Chrousos & Gold (1992).

What Psychobiological Abnormalities Exist for Those With PTSD?

Friedman and Yehuda are excellent sources for more detailed explanations of PTSD psychobiology.[121-123]

Research indicates that those with PTSD have abnormalities in certain brain structures as well as abnormalities in adrenergic, HPA, serotonergic and CRF mechanisms.

Alterations in Brain Structure

Advanced neuroimaging techniques show brain abnormalities among adults and children with PTSD. Specifically, reductions in hippocampal volume are seen in adults with PTSD.[124] The hippocampus is an important brain structure involved in information processing, learning, and memory. Children with PTSD also show abnormal brain development. They exhibit smaller *intracranial* and *intracerebral* volumes than children without PTSD.[125]

intracranial — within the vault of the skull

intracerebral — within the hemispheres of the brain

Adrenergic System

For those with PTSD, research indicates that the adrenergic (and SNS) systems are much more active in both adults and children than in normal individuals.[119, 126] The most dramatic illustrations of this finding are experiments with psychological and pharmacological probes.

psychological probe — a visual or auditory stimulus reminiscent of a traumatic experience to which a person with PTSD is exposed. For motor vehicle accident survivors such as Mary T., typical probes might include:
- *The sound of a large truck*
- *The squeal of brakes*
- *The sight of a truck crashing into a car*
- *Someone reciting the details of her own terrible accident in which her husband was killed*

A *psychological probe* presents to the patient a stimulus reminiscent of his/her traumatic experience.[127-128] Under such conditions, Mary T. would experience excessive SNS activation exhibited by a rise in blood pressure, a racing heart rate, and other indications of heightened SNS physiological activity. Mary would also evidence abnormal elevations of blood or urinary norepinephrine as well as alterations in the brain's normal blood flow. Motor vehicle accident survivors who do not develop PTSD would not exhibit the heightened reactivity of SNS and brain adrenergic mechanisms shown by Mary T.

pharmacological probe — a drug that can activate psychobiological mechanisms involved in the stress response

A typical *pharmacological probe* is yohimbine, which causes excessive firing of adrenergic neurons.[129] Research with yohimbine indicates that the adrenergic system is abnormally sensitive in PTSD. Indeed, giving an intravenous dose of yohimbine to Mary T. might provoke a panic attack or even a flashback of the truck crashing into her car. Yohimbine does not produce this response in people without PTSD or without panic disorder. Yohimbine can affect blood flow in the brain, thereby demonstrating the abnormal adrenergic sensitivity of those with PTSD.[124]

HPA System

Although the normal human stress response is associated with elevated cortisol levels, people with PTSD react just the opposite. Their cortisol levels are lower than those without PTSD.[130] When first reported, this was considered a paradoxical and most unexpected finding.[131] Although scientists have struggled to come up with an explanation of this PTSD-related abnormality, one possibility is that the encounter with a traumatic stressor is such a momentous shock to the human organism that normal HPA function is completely disrupted. Another possibility is that people who develop PTSD have vulnerable HPA systems and that the traumatic event unmasks a biological abnormality that impairs the capacity to cope with catastrophic stress.[16]

Adults with PTSD can be differentiated from those without PTSD through the *dexamethasone suppression test (DST)*. A dose of dexamethasone that will suppress HPA activity in PTSD patients will not do so in normal subjects, while a dose that will suppress HPA activity in normal subjects will not do so in depressed patients. Thus, dexamethasone is a pharmacological probe that helps clinicians distinguish those with PTSD from normal; and normal from depressed subjects.[132]

Serotonergic System

Although PTSD research with the serotonergic system is much more preliminary than research with adrenergic or HPA mechanisms, serotonin apparently plays an important modulatory role on both systems. Serotonin, therefore, is a key component of the human stress response in its own right.[119] Clinical studies indicate that PTSD patients experience abnormalities in serotonergic mechanisms, and may exhibit panic attacks and flashbacks when taking MCCP (m-chloro-phenyl-piperazine, a pharmacological probe of the serotonergic system). Those without PTSD do not demonstrate these responses.

Corticotropin Releasing Factor (CRF)

The one published experiment on CRF validates that CRF (which serves a key role in the human stress response) is

PTSD psychobiology is much more complicated than described here. The present discussion has been restricted to the major systems altered in people with PTSD because those systems are most influenced by the drugs currently used for PTSD treatment.

dexamethasone suppression test (DST)
dexamethasone is from the same chemical class as cortisol, and like cortisol, it can reduce HPA axis activity by reducing CRF secretion. PTSD, normal, and depressed patients differ significantly in their sensitivity to dexamethasone

elevated in people with PTSD.[133] This finding is entirely consistent with the adrenergic and HPA abnormalities in PTSD described previously.

Neurotransmission

The following discussion provides an overview of how medications used to treat PTSD modify neurotransmission in serotonergic and adrenergic neurons.

neurotransmitters — *chemical messengers that transmit signals from one nerve cell to another to elicit physiological responses*

synaptic cleft — *is the space between one neuron and the next that must be traversed by neurotransmitters*

pre-synaptic neuron — *is the neuron that initiates neurotransmission by releasing the neurotransmitter into the synaptic cleft*

post-synaptic neuron — *is the downstream neuron that is the target of neurotransmission*

receptors — *membrane bound protein molecules with a highly specific shape that facilitates binding by neurotransmitters or drugs*

Neurons communicate by releasing *neurotransmitters* into the *synaptic cleft*. The *pre-synaptic neuron* is responsible for packaging, releasing, and delivering the neurotransmitter into the synapse, where it can diffuse across to the *post-synaptic neuron*. Neurotransmitters attach to a specific post-synaptic *receptor.* The neurotransmitter forms a temporary binding complex with the receptor, analogous to a "lock-and-key" formation.

Binding of the neurotransmitter to the receptor results in a chemical change that leads to a biological response, such as a behavior, a thought, or a reaction.

After their pre-synaptic release, most neurotransmitters are subsequently reabsorbed by a specialized reuptake site located on the pre-synaptic neuron. The reuptake mechanism is selective for serotonin or norepinephrine respectively. Various medications affect different parts of the neurotransmitter system, especially SSRIs, TCAs, and MAOIs (see below) which are antidepressant agents that act by enhancing serotonergic and/or adrenergic neurotransmission through different mechanisms.

Selective Serotonin Reuptake Inhibitors (SSRIs) are antidepressants that block this presynaptic reuptake site on serotonergic neurons. The result is that more serotonin remains available within the synaptic cleft to bind to post-synaptic receptors.

Tricyclic Antidepressants (TCAs) block the presynaptic reuptake of both serotonin and norepinephrine thereby enhancing both serotonergic and adrenergic transmission by making more neurotransmitter available to bind to post-synaptic receptors.

Monoamine Oxidase Inhibitors (MAOIs) are antidepressants that block the enzyme MAO, which destroys both serotonin and norepinephrine. By preventing this destruction, more serotonin and norepinephrine are available for presynaptic release and, therefore, for binding to postsynaptic serotonergic and adrenergic receptors, respectively.

What Medical Treatments Are Used for PTSD?

Figure 4.2 (on pages 72-73) summarizes information from the current literature on medication trials, including drug class, specific medications, therapeutic dose range, clinical indications, and contraindications. For clinical indications, target symptoms identified are grouped as follows: [134]

- B Symptoms: instrusive recollections
- C Symptoms: avoidant/numbing
- D Symptoms: hyperarousal

This section reviews the research conducted for each class of drug available for PTSD treatment, and proven efficacy. The drug classes for PTSD treatment include:

- Selective Serotonin Reuptake Inhibitors (SSRIs)
- Monoamine Oxidase Inhibitors (MAOIs)
- Tricyclic Antidepressants (TCAs)
- Anti-adrenergic Agents
- Antianxiety Agents
- Anticonvulsants
- Antipsychotics

As we learn more about different brain mechanisms affected by PTSD, we can expect that new medications will be developed to act on other systems besides adrenergic, serotonergic, HPA, and CRF systems.

Selective Serotonin Reuptake Inhibitors (SSRIs)

To date, SSRIs are the most extensively investigated and most effective medications for treating PTSD. One SSRI (Sertraline) has Federal Drug Administration (FDA) approval for the treatment of PTSD. Most SSRI medication trials lasted 5-12 weeks with improvement found in 40 to 85 percent of respondents across trials. Noteworthy results indicate that SSRIs have a broad spectrum of actions with all three clusters (reexperiencing, avoidant/numbing, and hyperarousal) of PTSD symptoms significantly reduced by SSRI treatment in people traumatized by rape, criminal assault, and motor vehicle accidents.[134]

Sertraline is the best studied SSRI, having been found effective in two mulit-site randomized trials, each with approximately 200 patients.

Figure 4.2 — Evidence for Efficacy of Medications in the Treatment of PTSD

Based on the Published Literature (modified from Friedman, Davidson, Mellman & Southwick [134])

Drug Class	Specific Medications	Daily Dose	Indications	Contraindications
SSRI - Selective Serotonin Reuptake Inhibitors	Sertraline Fluoxetine Paroxetine Fluvoxamine	50-200 mg 20-80 mg 10-40 mg 250-300 mg	• Reduce B, C, & D symptoms • Produce Clinical Global Improvement • Effective Treatment for Depression, Panic Disorder, and Obsessive Compulsive Disorder • Reduce Associated Symptoms (rage, aggression, impulsivity, suicidal thoughts)	• May produce insomnia, restlessness, nausea, decreased appetite, daytime sedation, nervousness, and anxiety • May produce sexual dysfunction, such as decreased libido, delayed orgasm, or anorgasmia • May produce clinically significant drug interactions when prescribed to people taking MAOIs or other drugs for other medical conditions
Other Serotonergic Antidepressants	Trazadone Nefazadone	25-500 mg 100-600 mg	• May reduce B, C, & D symptoms. • Trazadone is synergistic with SSRIs & reverses SSRI-induced insomnia • Effective antidepressants; few side effects	• May be too sedating
MAOI - Monoamine Oxidase Inhibitor	Phenelzine	45-75 mg	• Reduces B symptoms • Produces Global Improvement • Effective Antidepressant and Antipanic Agent	• Patients must follow a strict dietary regimen or they may have a dangerous elevation in blood pressure (i.e., a hypertensive crisis). • Contraindicated in patients with alcohol/substance abuse/dependency • May produce insomnia, hypotension, anticholinergic and severe liver toxicity
TCA - Tricyclic Antidepressants	Imipramine Amitriptyline Desipramine	150-300 mg 150-300 mg 150-300 mg	• Reduce B Symptoms • Produce Global Improvement • Effective Antidepressant & Antipanic Agents	• Anticholinergic side effects (dry mouth, rapid pulse, blurred vision, constipation) • May produce abnormal electrocardiogram • May produce hypotension (low blood pressure), arousal, or sedation
Anti-adrenergic Agents	Clonidine Propranolol	0.2-0.6 mg 40-160 mg	• Reduce B & D Symptoms • Reduce B & D Symptoms	• May lower blood pressure or slow pulse rate too much • Must use cautiously with patients on hypotensive medications • Propranolol may produce depressive symptoms or psychomotor slowing

Evidence for Efficacy of Medications in the Treatment of PTSD continued

Drug Class	Specific Medications	Daily Dose	Indications	Contraindications
Antianxiety Agents	Alprazolam Clonazepam	0.5-6 mg 1-6 mg	• Reduce D Symptoms Only • Effective Anxiolytics & Antipanic Agents	• Should not be prescribed to patients with past or present alcohol/drug abuse/dependency • May exacerbate depressive symptoms
Anticonvulsants	Carbamazepine Valproate	600-1000 mg 750-1750 mg	• Effective on B & D Symptoms • Effective in Bipolar Affective Disorder • Effective on C & D Symptoms • Effective in Bipolar Affective Disorder	• May produce neurological symptoms, low sodium, and blood abnormalities through bone marrow toxicity • May produce gastrointestinal problems & tremor
Conventional Antipsychotics / Atypical Antipsychotics	Thioridazine Clozapine Risperidone	200-800 mg 300-900 mg 4-12 mg	• Sedation, hypotension, & anticholinergic affects • Extrapyramidal effects (thioridazine primarily)	• Possible effectiveness on B & D Symptoms • Effective Antipsychotic Agents

LEGEND

B Symptoms: intrusive recollections

C Symptoms: avoidant/numbing

D Symptoms: hyperarousal

SSRIs are also an attractive choice because they effectively treat disorders that are frequently comorbid with PTSD (e.g., depression, Panic Disorder, Obsessive-Compulsive Disorder, and Alcohol Dependence).

Finally, SSRIs may be clinically useful because a number of PTSD-associated symptoms may be mediated by serotonergic mechanisms. These include rage, impulsivity, suicidal intent, depressed mood, panic symptoms, and obsessional thinking. [135-136]

Clinicians should exercise caution when prescribing SSRIs to patients taking MAOIs or other medications. Serious drug interactions can occur due to SSRI-induced disruption of normal drug metabolism in the liver. Patients with gastrointestinal

Despite the clinical advantages of SSRIs and their relatively low side-effect profile in comparison with other antidepressant agents (e.g., MAOIs and TCAs), they are not tolerated by all patients. The sexual dysfunction, agitation, and insomnia produced by SSRIs, especially fluoxetine, may be especially disruptive to PTSD patients.

disorders, especially Irritable Bowel Syndrome, sometimes experience problems when taking SSRIs because of increased intestinal motility.

Other Serotonergic Antidepressants

Trazadone and nefazadone are antidepressants that have SSRI as well as other actions that enhance serotonergic synaptic actions. They have been tested very little but have shown some efficacy in clinical trials with PTSD patients.[137-138] Trazadone has recently received renewed attention because of its capacity to reverse the insomnia caused by SSRI agents such as fluoxetine and sertraline. As a result, many PTSD patients receiving SSRI treatment also receive trazadone at bedtime. Trazadone's advantage over conventional *hypnotics* is that its major serotonergic mode of action is synergistic with overall SSRI treatment and its sedative properties promote sleep.

hypnotics— *medications that promote sleep*

Monoamine Oxidase Inhibitors (MAOIs)

Comprehensive reviews of all published findings on MAOI treatment indicate that MAOIs produce moderate-to-good global improvement in 82 percent of patients.[139-140] This occurs primarily due to reduction in reexperiencing symptoms (e.g., intrusive recollections, traumatic nightmares, and PTSD flashbacks). Insomnia also improves. No improvement was found, however, in PTSD avoidant/numbing or hyperarousal symptoms.

One study of military combat veterans found that achieving positive clinical results took a minimum of eight weeks of treatment with MAOIs.

MAOI use has traditionally been limited when:

- There are legitimate concerns that patients may ingest alcohol.

- Patients may take pharmacologically contraindicated or illicit medications.

- Patients may not adhere to necessary dietary restrictions.

Though MAOIs have been tested infrequently, they have been highly effective in most reported drug trials. Since they are also excellent antidepressants and antipanic agents, further research is definitely warranted.

The most serious consequence of noncompliance (such as use of illicit medications, alcohol, or ingestion of contraindicated foods), is severe and abrupt elevation of blood pressure (hypertensive crisis), which is a medical emergency.

Tricyclic Antidepressants (TCAs)

TCAs are not as effective for treating PTSD for three reasons. First, an analysis of all published findings on TCA treatment for PTSD found that only 45 percent of patients showed moderate to good global improvement following treatment.[140] In contrast, 82 percent of those taking MAOIs experienced global improvement. Second, there is a lack of potency. As with MAOIs, most improvement resulted from reductions in reexperiencing rather than avoidant/numbing or arousal symptoms. In addition, research with military combat veterans indicates that TCA's also take a minimum of 8 weeks of treatment to achieve positive clinical results. Third, TCAs' anticholinergic, hypotensive, sedating, and cardiac arrhythmic side effects are not tolerated well by many PTSD patients.

Recent testing with a much safer MAOI, moclobemide suggests that this drug may prove to be effective for PTSD.

TCAs' relative lack of potency, side effects, and failure to reduce avoidant/ numbing symptoms have led clinicians to rely more heavily on SSRIs as first-line drugs in PTSD treatment.[134]

Anti-adrenergic Agents: Propranolol and Clonidine

Research indicates that the adrenergic system functions abnormally in those with chronic PTSD.[119] Therefore, it is surprising that there has been so little research with two medications that reduce excessive adrenergic activity, propranolol and clonidine. Propranolol is a post-synaptic blocking agent that prevents norepinephrine from binding with the receptor. Clonidine acts presynaptically where it reduces the amount of adrenergic neurotransmitter released.

Existing research includes three reports on propranolol and four on clonidine. In the best scientific study on propranolol, it was administered to 11 physically and/or sexually abused children with PTSD in an A-B-A design (six weeks off; six weeks on; six weeks off medication). Researchers observed significant reductions (25-64 percent) in reexperiencing and arousal symptoms during drug treatment, but symptoms relapsed to pre-treatment severity following medication discontinuation. Two other published reports on propranolol treatment for PTSD have had mixed results.[141]

Results from four reports with clonidine indicate successful reduction in 15-50 percent of PTSD associated symptoms, such as:
- Traumatic nightmares
- Intrusive recollections
- Hypervigilance
- Insomnia
- Startle reactions
- Angry outbursts

Three different clinical populations participated in the trials with clonidine treatment: Vietnam veterans, abused children, and Cambodian refugees.[141]

In addition, patients in these trials reported improved mood and concentration. As with propranolol, more extensive clonidine testing than these preliminary reports is needed to conclusively demonstrate PTSD treatment efficacy.

Antianxiety Agents

benzodiazepine family of medication— *a very effective and widely prescribed class of drugs for anxiety that includes diazepam, lorazepam, alprazolam, and clonazepam*

A serious withdrawal syndrome has been reported following abrupt discontinuation of alprazolam among PTSD patients.[23]

Research results with anticonvulsants can only be considered preliminary at this time. Large-scale trials with these (and other newly developed anticonvulsants) are needed to clarify their usefulness in PTSD treatment.

Antianxiety agents (in the *benzodiazepine family of medication*) have been prescribed widely for PTSD patients in some clinical settings, although they have not been extensively tested in formal research protocols. In a well-controlled randomized clinical trial with alprazolam and in other studies, no improvement was observed in core PTSD reexperiencing, avoidant, or numbing symptoms.[142] However, patients reported reduced insomnia, anxiety, and irritability, an expected outcome due to nonspecific antianxiety effects.

Anticonvulsants

Researchers hypothesize that following exposure to traumatic events, certain nuclei in the brain become progressively "kindled" or "sensitized" so that subsequently these nuclei exhibit excessive responsivity to less-intense, trauma-related stimuli.[143] As a result, various research trials have been conducted using anticonvulsant/antikindling medications with PTSD patients. In five studies, carbamazepine produced 50-75 percent reductions in reexperiencing and arousal symptoms. In three studies, valproate produced 60-75 percent reductions in avoidant/numbing symptoms and 50-65 percent reduction in arousal (but not reexperiencing) symptoms.[141]

hematopoietic — *suppression of the bone marrow's capacity to produce red and white blood cells*

teratogenic — *producing fetal abnormalities during pregnancy*

However, these medications have a clinically significant spectrum of neurological, *hematopoietic*, gastrointestinal, and *teratogenic* side effects that may restrict their usefulness for a number of patients. The theoretical importance of the kindling/sensitization model of PTSD warrants more extensive study of such anticonvulsant agents.

Antipsychotics

psychotic disorder — *mental disorder characterized by gross impairment in perceptions of reality*

Before the empirical and conceptual advances achieved during the past 15 years, PTSD patients were often considered to have a *psychotic disorder* because of their intense agitation, hypervigilance/paranoia, impulsivity, and *dissociative states*. Times have changed, however, and the current thinking is that most of these symptoms will respond to anti-adrenergic or antidepressant medications.

However, for the rare PTSD patient who exhibits psychotic symptoms, clinicians have prescribed anti-psychotic medications.[141] Recently, clinicians have begun to prescribe the newly developed atypical antipsychotics for PTSD patients, such as risperidone, olanzepine, and quetiapine. Preliminary anecdotal observations with these medications suggest that they may have unique applicability for hypervigilant/paranoid, isolated, aggressive, agitated, or psychotic PTSD patients unresponsive to other medications.[134] Clinicians should be cautious with these newer medications since their usefulness in PTSD treatment has not been established by well-controlled drug trials.

dissociative states — *mental states characterized by a break down between normally integrated psychological functioning of consciousness, perception of self, and sensory/motor behavior*

What is a Good Strategy for PTSD Pharmacotherapy?

SSRIs are the first line treatment for PTSD because they perform better than other agents in drug trials and because serotonergic mechanisms appear to mediate core PTSD (B, C, and D) symptoms. Some patients who neither benefit from SSRIs nor can tolerate their side effects deserve a trial of TCAs (since they are more safely and easily administered than MAOIs). Beyond this, there are no clear guidelines for clinicians. Treatment decisions need to consider specific symptoms as well as comorbid disorders, such as:

Recommendations regarding pharmacotherapy are based on the author's interpretation of literature, an understanding of how these drugs work, and personal clinical experience.

- **For patients with impulsivity, mood lability, irritability, aggressiveness, and suicidal behavior** select an SSRI. Serotonergic mechanisms also appear to help in comorbid disorders (e.g., depression, Panic Disorder, Obsessive-Compulsive Disorder, and alcohol/drug abuse/dependency).

- **For patients who are excessively aroused or hyperreactive**, SSRI treatment may be supplemented with the anti-adrenergic agents, clonidine, guanfacine, or propranolol, which often reduce hyperarousal and reexperiencing symptoms. Furthermore, decreasing adrenergic activity is often accompanied by dramatic reductions in dissociative symptoms (which appear to be an extreme manifestation of PTSD hyperarousal).

With clonidine guanfacine, or propranolol, the clinician will usually know after one or two weeks whether an anti-adrenergic agent will be beneficial. This is a much shorter time frame than with almost any other psychotropic agents, which usually requires four to eight weeks before demonstrating efficacy.

- **For labile, impulsive, and/or aggressive patients**, anticonvulsant/antikindling agents may be useful.

Because PTSD rarely appears as a unitary syndrome, the choice of which drug to prescribe will necessarily include consideration of that drug's efficacy against the comorbid disorder as well as against PTSD.

- **For fearful, paranoid, hypervigilent, and psychotic patients**, atypical antipsychotics may be helpful.

- **For patients with comorbid Major Depressive Disorder,** one would be more likely to select an SSRI, TCA, or MAOI rather than propranolol since the former group of medications are also potent antidepressant agents. Propranolol is also known to produce depressive symptoms in susceptible patients.

- **For patients with PTSD and alcohol/drug dependence**, avoid prescribing an MAOI since the adverse interaction between the MAOI and alcohol, cocaine, or some other illicit drug could produce serious side effects. Rather, significant reductions in both PTSD symptoms and alcohol consumption have been observed following sertraline treatment among subjects who have comorbid PTSD and alcohol dependence.[135] This is an important finding because of high comorbidity rates among those treatment-seeking patients with PTSD and alcohol abuse/dependence.

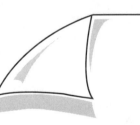

*Therapy Notes
from the Desk
of Pat Owen*

August 28

She's responding well to SSRI treatment. Resistant at first, but fortunately had few side effects. The medication has complemented CBT treatment by promoting further reductions in intrusive, avoidant, and numbing symptoms. She's achieving better SUDS reduction in CBT and functioning better at home. Comorbid depressive and panic symptoms also better since SSRI began. She still exhibits too much hyperarousal. I may have to add an anti-adrenergic agent in a few more weeks if she shows no further improvement.

Appendix A: PTSD Assessment Tools for Adults

Clinicians have a number of diagnostic instruments to choose from, falling into three overlapping categories:

1. Trauma Exposure Scales (Criterion A_1)

2. Diagnostic Instruments

3. Assessment of PTSD Symptom Severity (Criteria B, C, and D)

Trauma Exposure Scales

Traumatic exposure scales can be divided into those that inquire about exposure to all possible kinds of traumatic experiences and those that focus on a specific kind of trauma. For example, specific scales have been developed to assess child abuse, domestic violence, rape, war-zone exposure, and torture.

General Traumatic Experiences

Traumatic Stress Schedule (TSS) — A brief, self-report screening questionnaire that covers nine classes of traumatic events:

1. Robbery

2. Physical assault

3. Sexual assault

4. Loss of a loved one through accident/homicide/suicide

5. Personal injury

6. Property loss due to a disaster

7. Forced evacuation due to imminent danger or environmental hazard

8. Motor vehicle accident causing serious injury

9. Other "terrifying or shocking" experiences

The TSS has good *reliability* and is quick and easy to administer, but it has only one question for each class of traumatic events.[144]

reliability — the extent to which the test produces similar results when administered at different times

79 © Compact Clinicals

Potential Stressful Experiences Inventory (PSEI) — A self-report scale that measures lifetime exposure to a wide variety of traumatic experiences. PSEI assesses traumatic and non-traumatic events categorized as "high-" and "low-magnitude" stressors. Since the PSEI obtains information about both objective and subjective aspects of traumatic experiences, it helps clinicians assess both Criterion A_1 and A_2 for each identified event. Finally, the PSEI inquires about the first, most recent, and worst high-magnitude event.[145]

Traumatic Events Questionnaire (TEQ) — A self-report instrument that assesses 11 specific traumatic events. Specific probes inquire about life threat or injury associated with the trauma. TEQ has excellent *test-retest reliability*.[146]

*test-retest reliability —
the extent to which those
tested obtain similar
scores each time they take
the test*

Evaluation of Lifetime Stressors (ELS) — Designed as a clinically sensitive instrument that is comprehensive in scope and optimizes traumatic experience reporting, the ELS is a two stage instrument, beginning with a self-report questionnaire and ending with a structured clinician interview. The ELS was constructed to ask both broad and detailed questions in a clinically sensitive way that does not provoke avoidant behavior or answers that might minimize clients' responses on the emotional impact of traumatic experiences.[147]

Specific Traumatic Experiences

Childhood Trauma

Child Abuse and Trauma Scale — A self-report measure for adults that assesses the frequency and intensity of various adverse experiences during childhood and adolescence. It provides a quantitative index of the experience severity. This report has been tested on two large samples of college students and has been shown to have strong *internal consistency* and good test-retest reliability.[148]

*internal consistency —
the degree to which various
parts of a test measure
the same variables*

Childhood Trauma Questionnaire — A comprehensive, self-report scale for adults that assesses four independent factors: physical and emotional abuse, emotional neglect, sexual abuse, and physical neglect. This questionnaire has high internal consistency and good test-retest reliability.[149]

Familial Experiences Inventory — A comprehensive, clinician-administered diagnostic interview for adults that assesses childhood physical abuse, sexual abuse, and neglect.

Clinicians can use this inventory to obtain information on each traumatic experience's frequency, severity, duration, and impact. [150]

Retrospective Assessment of Traumatic Experiences (RATE) — A comprehensive instrument that addresses parental separation and loss as well as extrafamilial and familial abuse, childhood abuse and neglect. The assessments cover frequency, intensity, and duration of trauma. [151]

Early Trauma Inventory (ETI) — A highly comprehensive and detailed clinical interview to assess childhood emotional, physical, and sexual abuse as well as non-abusive traumas. Formatted like a clinical interview, each subsection begins with an open-ended inquiry about traumatic events that progresses to a series of detailed questions. The ETI inquires about perpetration, victim age, frequency (at different developmental periods), and subjective response at the time of the trauma as well as the interview. [152]

Domestic Violence

Conflict Tactics Scale (CTS) — One of the first scales of this nature designed to assess partner abuse, CTS is a widely used self-report subscale on verbal aggression and violence within the family. [153]

Abusive Behavior Inventory (ABI) — In addition to verbal aggression and partner violence assessed by the CTS, the ABI self-report instrument also assesses physical injury, psychological abuse, and terrorism without physical assault within a domestic context. ABI offers acceptable reliability and *validity*. [154]

validity — *the extent to which the instrument actually measures what it claims*

Sexual Experiences Survey (SES) — A self-report instrument designed to identify rape victims and perpetrators within a normal (in contrast to a treatment-seeking) population. SES has good reliability and validity. [155]

Wyatt Sex History Questionnaire (WSHQ) — A structured interview, administered by a clinician, for assessing coercive vs. consensual sexual experiences. One attribute of this instrument is that it has been *standardized* on a multi-ethnic sample of women. [156]

standardized — *data collected on a large group and results put in the form of averages by age and group*

War-zone Trauma

Combat Exposure Scale (CES) — This widely used, self-report scale was standardized with Vietnam veterans but has been adapted for use with veterans of other conflicts (e.g., Persian Gulf War, Somalia, Bosnia). CES has good internal consistency and test-retest reliability. [157]

Women's Wartime Stressor Scale (WWSS) — Developed as a self-report instrument to assess unique aspects of war-zone exposure relevant to the experience of female Vietnam veterans, this scale also assesses sexual trauma and nursing-related events. WWSS has good *psychometric properties*. [158]

psychometric properties
— the elements of constructing a useful instrument such as establishing reliability and validity

Torture

Harvard Trauma Questionnaire (HTQ) — Developed to assess torture, trauma, and PTSD among Indochinese refugees, HTQ is a culturally sensitive self-report instrument. It has both open-ended and detailed questions in which respondents report on their own worst experiences as well as about torture experiences they witnessed or heard about.[159]

Diagnostic Instruments

Diagnostic scales are used as either structured clinical interviews (administered by a clinician) or as lay interviews designed for epidemiological research. A number of self-report PTSD symptom severity scores can be used for diagnostic purposes (see PTSD Severity Scales on page 23). In these instances, people with higher scores may be considered to have PTSD. In general, it is best to conduct a systematic diagnostic assessment. The Clinician Administered PTSD Scale (CAPS), reviewed on the next page, was designed by the National Center for PTSD as both a diagnostic and symptom severity instrument.

Structured Clinical Interview for DSM-IV (SCID): PTSD module — The SCID provides a comprehensive DSM-IV diagnostic assessment with a separate module for each *Axis I disorder*. Therefore, it is not only useful for diagnosing PTSD but also for diagnosing any possible comorbid disorder. SCID must be administered by a trained clinician since it is a structured interview with a number of probes designed to elicit

Axis I disorder — diagnoses listed in the DSM (Diagnostic and Statistical Manual of Mental Disorders) that are major psychiatric disorders

relevant clinical information. It is used widely and has performed well. The major limitation of the SCID is that it only provides dichotomous (yes/no) information about the presence or absence of each symptom. Though it determines the nature of a traumatic experience, it does not measure the exposure severity. Therefore, although the SCID is the "gold standard" for diagnostic assessment, it can neither provide information about symptom severity nor can it detect any changes in symptom severity following treatment. [160]

Clinician Administered PTSD Scale (CAPS) — Designed as a quantitative expansion of the SCID, PTSD module is a structured interview designed to monitor treatment response and must be administered by a trained clinician. Criteria A_1 and A_2 are assessed before inquiring about B, C, and D symptoms. Also, like the SCID, it provides information on both current and lifetime PTSD. Unlike the SCID, CAPS provides a continuous measure of each PTSD (and associated) symptom along two dimensions: intensity and frequency. Therefore, the total PTSD severity score is the sum of the separate intensity and frequency scores. CAPS has become the instrument of choice in drug or psychotherapy treatment research. It has excellent psychometric properties. [161]

PTSD-Interview — A diagnostic instrument that also measures PTSD symptom severity, this interview differs from the previously mentioned assessment tools because it was designed for administration by lay interviewers rather than by trained clinicians. The client rather than the clinician makes his/her own rating of symptom severity. Thus, it is more a self-report instrument than a structured interview administered by an experienced clinician. [162]

The Davidson Self-Rating PTSD Scale — A 17-item, self-report measure that is based on the PTSD symptom clusters defined by DSM-IV. Each item is rated from 0 to 4 for both frequency and severity during the previous week. Items are summed for a total score and subscales of reexperiencing, avoidance, and arousal. The total scale has demonstrated good test-retest reliability and internal consistency. The subscales also seem more reliable than the SCID for diagnosing PTSD.

Composite International Diagnostic Interview (CIDI) — A structured diagnostic interview for all DSM-IV diagnoses designed for survey research employing lay rather than clinician interviewers. The PTSD module has good *sensitivity* and *specificity*. The CIDI was used in the National Comorbidity

The SCID provides information about the presence of both current or lifetime diagnoses so clinicians can determine whether or not someone who currently does not meet DSM-IV criteria for PTSD may have done so at some time in the past.

A growing trend has been to use the SCID for a comprehensive diagnostic assessment but to substitute the CAPS for the SCID PTSD module to simultaneously carry out PTSD diagnostic assessment and measure PTSD symptom severity.

The PTSD-Interview more closely resembles the Davidson Self-Rating PTSD Scale or CIDI.

sensitivity — *percent of cases correctly identified by the instrument*

specificity — *percent of non-cases correctly identified by the instrument*

Study (see Chapter 2: pages 24 and 25) and currently is the instrument of choice for epidemiologic research concerning PTSD.[164]

Diagnostic Interview Schedule IV (DIS-IV) — a structured diagnostic interview (like the CIDI) designed to be administered by experienced lay interviewers without clinical training.[165] The DIS has been used in psychiatric survey research for decades to assess the prevalence of psychiatric disorders in the general population. Although it is being displaced in some quarters by the CIDI, it is still an excellent instrument. The PTSD module of the DIS-IV has good sensitivity and specificity.[166]

PTSD Symptom Severity Scales

PTSD Checklist (PCL) — A self-report questionnaire that assesses the 17 PTSD symptoms on a five-point scale. PCL has good sensitivity and specificity, and it correlates well with other standard measures. To date, PCL has been primarily used in research with combat veterans.[167]

PTSD Symptom Scale (PSS) — A self-report questionnaire that assesses the 17 PTSD symptoms on a four-point scale. PSS has excellent psychometric properties and has been used mostly with rape victims.[168]

correlates — the degree to which two scores are systematically related to each other: "co-relate"

PK-Scale of the MMPI-2 — A 49-item subscale of the MMPI-2, this scale has been used mostly with veterans but has performed well with rape victims and other traumatized groups. It *correlates* well with the CAPS. Its advantage is that since it is a subscale of the MMPI, the PK-Scale can be extracted from the entire MMPI when the MMPI-2 is administered routinely. Possible disadvantages include its length and its track record for not always performing as well as other instruments for assessing PTSD symptom severity.[169]

predictive validity — the extent to which scores on an instrument predict actual performance

PS-Scale of the MMPI-2 — Like the PK Scale, the PS-Scale was originally developed for epidemiological research with Vietnam veterans. However, it may have broader applicability to other traumatized groups (e.g., child abuse, criminal victimization) but has only moderate *predictive validity* and has not been studied extensively.[170]

Symptom Checklist-PTSD (SCL-PTSD) — A 28-item scale that can be extracted from the 90-item, self-report *Symptom Checklist-90 (SCL-90)*, the SCL-PTSD was standardized on women with a history of criminal victimization. It is not as well validated as some of the other scales but has the advantage (like the PK-MMPI-2 scale) that it can be extracted from an assessment instrument that is widely used. [171]

Impact of Event Scale-Revised (IES-R) — A revision of a self-report scale that was widely used in PTSD assessment, the IES-R consists of 22 items that tap Criterion B, C, and D symptoms, each rated on a five-point scale. IES-R was originally tested on natural disaster survivors and has performed quite well. [172]

Mississippi Scale for Combat-Related PTSD (M-PTSD) — A 35-item instrument developed for combat veterans that, in addition to Criterion B, C, and D symptoms, taps associated symptoms such as guilt and suicidality. The M-PTSD has performed extremely well in research and clinical settings. [173]

Civilian Mississippi Scale — Modified from the M-PTSD and designed for non-veterans, this scale has been used mostly with civilian survivors of natural disasters. Reliability and validity results have been mixed. [174]

Penn Inventory — This 26-item scale was developed and validated on both veterans and civilians (disaster survivors). It has exhibited high sensitivity and specificity but has not been extensively tested. [175]

Trauma Symptom Checklist-40 (TSC-40) — Developed specifically for use with adult survivors of childhood sexual abuse, the TSC-40 subscales tap anxiety, depression, dissociation, postsexual abuse trauma, and sleep disturbance. It has been used mostly with young adult men and women, and it has performed well. [176]

Trauma Symptom Inventory (TSI) — This instrument expands the TSC-40 to a 100-item instrument with 10 subscales that tap anxiety, depression, anger, PTSD symptoms, sexual concerns/behavior, and dissociation. TSI correlates well with other PTSD scales and has been useful as both a clinical and research tool. [177]

Symptom Checklist-90 (SCL-90) — a broad-spectrum instrument that assesses many different psychological domains, including depressive, psychotic, and anxiety symptoms

---

Symptom Severity Scales for
Acute Stress Disorder (ASD)

Acute Stress Reaction Questionnaire (ASRQ) — A 35-item, self-report questionnaire in which respondents rate their experiences during and shortly after traumatic event on a five-point scale.[178] Seventeen items focus on dissociative symptoms such as psychic numbing, stupor, derealization, depersonalization, detachment, estrangement from others, amnesia, and flashbacks. The other items focus on intrusion, avoidance, and arousal symptoms. ASRQ has good internal consistency, but has not been widely utilized.

Peritraumatic Dissociative Experiences Questionnaire (PDEQ) — A 10-item questionnaire (that has both self-report and clinician versions) in which dissociative symptoms are ranked on a three-point scale.[179] Items assess:

- losing track of time (blanking out)
- functioning on "automatic pilot"
- experiencing a distorted sense of time
- derealization
- depersonalization
- not feeling pain associated with injury

The PDEQ has been tested on female Vietnam veterans, earthquake survivors, and emergency medical personnel with good reliability and validity.

Appendix B: PTSD Assessment Tools for Children

As with adults, scales for assessing and diagnosing PTSD in children can be divided into the three overlapping categories:

1. Trauma Exposure Scale (Criterion A_1)

2. Diagnostic Instruments

3. Assessment of PTSD Symptom Severity

Key things to remember about scales for children are:

- They must be developmentally sensitive.

- They must be worded so that they can be easily understood.

- They typically have companion scales for parents or teachers.

- It is inadvisable to administer questionnaires to children younger than six, since they lack the verbal and cognitive abstracting ability to understand questions and to respond appropriately.

More detailed information on all of these scales can be found in Kathleen Nader's recent book chapter on assessing traumatic experiences in children.[180]

Trauma Exposure Scales

My Worst Experience Survey (MWES) and **My Worst School Experience Survey (MWSES)** — These are both lengthy interviews that must be administered by a skilled clinician. They assess the child's most stressful experiences either in the general environment or specifically in the school setting. Such stressors include: abuse, assault, disaster, death of loved one, parental separation, or family problems. These surveys also systematically address the emotional response to such stressors so that Criterion A_2 can also be assessed.[181]

Traumatic Event Screening Instrument (TESI) — The TESI has child and parent (TESI-C and TESI-P) versions, respectively. It is a 15-item, broad-spectrum interview that must be administered by a trained clinician. The TESI inquires about accidents, disasters, hospitalizations, physical abuse, sexual abuse, and exposure to domestic or other violent events. It is still being developed and has not been subjected to validity or reliability testing.[182]

When Bad Things Happen Scale (WBTHS) — This is a self-report diagnostic instrument that has four associated scales, one of which, the Dimensions of Stressful Events (DOSE), measures Criterion A events. (The other accompanying scales are an interview with the child, a parent interview, and a parent questionnaire regarding the child).[180] WBTHS has been used with Armenian, Israeli, and American children with preliminary data suggesting good validity and reliability. The World Health Organization (WHO) and Centers for Disease Control (CDC) provide computer programs for scoring and analyzing the WBTH.[183]

Children's Sexual Behavior Inventory 3 (CSBI-3) — This instrument is a simply worded, 36-item questionnaire that can be administered by parents or primary care givers.[184] CSBI-3 assesses the frequency of a wide variety of sexual behaviors on a four-point scale, including traumatic and non-traumatic (e.g., self-stimulation and voluntary activities with others). The inventory has been translated into French, Spanish, German, and Swedish. Research with the CSBI-3 indicates that it can distinguish sexually abused from non-abused children. Those familiar with its use recommend that CSBI-3 is best used "as part of a comprehensive evaluation…with careful clinical interviewing and assessment of other behavior problems." [180 (page 335)]

Child Rating Scales of Exposure to Interpersonal Abuse (CRS-EIA) and **The Angie/Andy CRS (A/A CRS)** — These are clinician-administered scales to assess the frequency and severity of exposure to interpersonal abuse by 6-11 year olds. [180, 185-186] The questionnaire used consists of cartoons depicting sexual abuse, physical abuse, or witnessing family or community violence. The A/A is designed for girls (Angie) and boys (Andy) so that the cartoons are gender-appropriate for the child being assessed. There is also a companion A/A PRS for parents, which is keyed to the A/A CRS and has verbal items rather than cartoons. This instrument is still being revised, but has performed well in preliminary trials. Researchers expect that these scales will also be useful for assessing complex PTSD as well as DSM-IV PTSD.

My Exposure to Violence (My-ETV) — This is a structured interview designed for children, adolescents and young adults (ages 9 to 24) that measures both chronic and acute exposure to 18 different violent events that have either been witnessed or personally experienced. Items include: being shot, sexually assaulted, attacked with a weapon, seriously threatened, or witnessing a killing, shooting, rape, or assault. The My-ETV has high internal consistency, test-retest reliability, and construct validity.[187]

Diagnostic Instruments

As with adults, diagnostic instruments include structured clinical interviews to be administered by a clinician or lay interviews designed for epidemiological research. Self-report Symptom Severity Scales (see page 22) are sometimes used for diagnostic purposes as well. Again, as with adults, the Clinician-Administered PTSD Scale for children (CAPS-C) was designed as both a diagnostic and symptom severity scale.

Diagnostic Interview for Children and Adolescents-Revised (DICA-R) — This is the child equivalent of the SCID (see Appendix A).[180, 188] DICA-R is a broad-spectrum diagnostic interview designed to assess all DSM-IV diagnoses with a specific module dedicated to PTSD. There is a four-point rating for symptom severity that focuses on frequency rather than intensity. The PTSD module offers good *inter-rater reliability*, but its performance has been mixed with regard to specificity and sensitivity. Clinicians need to get appropriate training to administer this instrument effectively.

Clinician Administered PTSD Scale for Children (CAPS-C) — This scale is the child equivalent of the CAPS (see Appendix A).[180, 189] CAPS-C is a structured interview that assesses the severity (i.e., intensity plus frequency) of each PTSD symptom. It has performed well with good reliability and validity. There is a manual that accompanies the CAPS-C, and clinicians must receive training in order to use this instrument.

Diagnostic Interview Schedule for Children, version 2.3 (DISC) — This interview has been designed for epidemiological research (like the DIS or CIDI for adults - see Appendix A) with both child and parent versions.[180, 190] Preliminary results suggest that the PTSD module of the DISC may lack sufficient specificity and sensitivity to detect PTSD in community surveys.

PTSD Symptom Severity Scales

Child Post-Traumatic Stress Reaction Index (CPTS-RI) — This index is a 20-item, semi-structured interview for children and adolescents that has been successfully administered to a

For clinical assessment or research with children, clinicians typically might use the DICA-R to determine comorbid diagnoses and substitute the CAPS-C for the DICA-R PTSD module to simultaneously conduct PTSD diagnostic assessment and measure symptom severity.

Inter-rater reliability — the degree to which different raters agree on a diagnosis based on instrument use

variety of traumatized populations.[180, 191] There are child and parent versions that rate PTSD symptoms on a five-point scale. CPTS-RI has been translated into Cambodian, Arabic, Croatian, Armenian, and Norwegian and has good reliability and validity. It has performed well in research with children exposed to natural disasters, war and school-yard sniper attacks. Since CPTS-RI does not inquire about all PTSD symptoms, it cannot be used for diagnostic purposes; however, it is a good instrument for assessing PTSD severity.

Child's Reaction to Traumatic Events Scale (CRTES) — This scale is a revision of the Impact of Events Scale modified for children (see Appendix A) that focuses on intrusions and avoidance (but not hyperarousal) PTSD symptoms.[180, 192] CRTES is a brief, 15-item scale that is easy to administer. The CRTES is currently undergoing psychometric evaluation.

Children's Impact of Traumatic Events Scale (CITES) — This is a 78-item measure with four subscales: PTSD, Social Relations, Abuse Attributions, and Eroticism.[180, 193] CITES is a clinician-administered, semi-structured interview that assesses symptoms on a three-point scale. Correlations with other child abuse scales have been mixed, possibly because the CITES expands the inquiry beyond conventional post-abuse outcomes to assess social reactions and other subjective responses often exhibited by sexually abused children.

Trauma Symptom Checklist for Children (TSCC) — This checklist is a 54-item, self-report questionnaire for 8-16 year olds that assesses the effects of trauma with respect to PTSD, anxiety, depression, anger, and dissociation.[194-195] TSCC has good internal consistency and validity, is easy to use and cost effective, and can be completed by non-traumatized children within 20 minutes (traumatized children often require more time).

Child Dissociative Checklist (CDC) — This is a 20-item, easily administered, cost-effective instrument designed to assess dissociative symptoms in sexually abused children and adolescents.[180, 196] These symptoms include dissociative amnesia, rapid shifts in observable cognitive/behavioral indices, spontaneous trance states, hallucinations, alterations in identity, and aggressive/sexual behavior. CDC has excellent internal consistency and test-retest reliability. No training is required for administration.

Glossary

A

adrenergic response — *neuronal activation mediated by either noradrenaline or adrenaline*

affective lability — *rapid and unpredictable shifts in mood state*

amnesia — *mental syndrome characterized by partial or complete memory loss*

art therapy — *a treatment procedure in which clients express themselves through drawing, writing, dance, drama, or other creative media to access underlying emotions*

"ataques de nervios" — *a common symptom of distress among Hispanic American groups involving anxiety, uncontrollable shouting and crying, trembling, heart palpitations, difficulty moving limbs, difficulty breathing, dizziness, fainting spells, and dissociative symptoms such as amnesia and alteration of consciousness*

Axis I disorders — *diagnoses listed in the DSM (Diagnostic and Statistical Manual of Mental Disorders) that are major psychiatric disorders*

B

benzodiazepine family of drugs — *a very effective and widely prescribed class of drugs for anxiety that includes diazepam, lorazepam, alprazolam, and clonazepam*

Borderline Personality Disorder — *a personality disorder characterized by extreme instabilities fluctuating between normal functioning and psychic disability*

C

"calor" — *a stress-related syndrome observed among Salvadoran women described as a surge of intense heat that may rapidly spread throughout the entire body for a few moments or for several days*

cognitive behavioral approaches — *therapeutic approaches that focus on how patterns of thinking, are shaped by reinforcement, learning and conditioning models*

comorbid disorders — *major psychiatric disorders that are present at the same time an individual has full-fledged PTSD*

correlates — *the degree to which two scores are systematically related to each other: "co-relate"*

cortisol — *a hormone that increases energy by raising blood glucose levels, decreases immune processes, and has other metabolic and neurobiological actions*

countertransference — *the clinician's psychological reaction to something the client said or did*

D

depersonalization — *an alteration in the perception or experience of the self so that one feels detached from, and as if one is an outside observer of one's mental processes or body (e.g., feeling like one is in a dream)*

derealization — *an alteration in the perception or experience of the external world so that it seems strange or unreal (e.g., people may seem unfamiliar or mechanical; time may seem speeded up or slowed down)*

dexamethasone suppression test (DST) — *dexamethasone is from the same chemical class as cortisol, and like cortisol, it can reduce HPA axis activity by reducing CRF secretion. PTSD, normal, and depressed patients differ significantly in their sensitivity to dexamethasone.*

dissociation — *an abnormal psychological state in which one's perception of oneself and/or one's environment is altered significantly*

dissociative amnesia — *inability to recall an important aspect of the trauma*

Dissociative Identity Disorder — *a mental disorder characterized by one's personality becoming so fragmented that pronounced changes in behavior and reactivity are noticed between different social situations or social roles*

dissociative states — *mental states characterized by a break down between normally integrated psychological functioning of consciousness, perception of self, and sensory/motor behavior*

DSM-III — *Diagnostic and Statistical Manual of Mental Disorders - Third Edition published by the American Psychiatric Association and is the authoritative source on psychiatric diagnosis*

DSM-IV — *Diagnostic and Statistical Manual of mental Disorders-Fourth Edition*

E

epidemiological data — *research data on the aspects of diseases or disorders in the general population*

F

fragmented thoughts — *the inability to sustain continuity and coherence in one's cognitive processes*

flashback episode — *a dissociative state in which an individual feels as if he or she is reliving a traumatic event*

G

Generalized Anxiety Disorder — *a psychiatric disorder marked by unrealistic worry, apprehension, and uncertainty*

H

habituation — *gradual, naturally occurring reduction of anxiety or discomfort over time, if exposure is maintained*

hallucination — *sensory perceptions without external stimulation; hearing voices or seeing things others do not; a compelling perceptual experience of seeing, hearing, or smelling something that is not actually present*

hematopoietic — *suppression of the bone marrow's capacity to produce red and white blood cells*

hyper-reactive psychophysiological state — *a state in which emotions are heightened and aroused and even minor events may produce a state in which the heart pounds rapidly, muscles tense, and there is great overall agitation*

hypnotics — *medications that promote sleep*

hypothalamic-pituitary-adrenocortical (HPA) axis — *refers to three anatomic structures that participate collectively in hormonal response to stress: the hypothalamus (in the brain), the pituitary gland, and the outer layer (cortex) of the adrenal gland*

I

internal consistency — *the degree to which various parts of a test measure the same variables*

inter-rater reliability — *the degree to which different raters agree on a diagnosis based on instrument use*

intracerebral — *within the hemispheres of the brain*

intracranial — *within the vault of the skull*

M

Million Clinical Multiaxial Inventory (MCMI) — *an instrument for assessing mental disorders, developed for use with hospitalized psychiatric clients*

Minnesota Multiphasic Personality Inventory (MMPI) — *a widely used instrument for mental disorders, assessing personality and symptoms of distress*

N

neurotransmitters — *chemical messengers that transmit signals from one nerve cell to another to elicit physiological responses*

neutrality — *a psychoanalytic technique by which clinicians reveal as little of themselves as possible so that thoughts, memories, and feelings generated during therapy come from the client's intrapsychic processes rather than from an interpersonal relationship between client and clinician*

P

Panic Disorder — *a psychiatric disorder marked by intense anxiety and panic including symptoms such as palpitations, shortness of breath, sweating*

pathological changes — *changes resulting in an abnormal condition that prevents proper psychological functioning*

personality pathology — *maladaptive pattern of relating to other people that severely impairs social functioning and adaptive potential*

peritraumatic dissociation — *dissociation during and shortly after the trauma*

pharmacological probe — *a drug which can activate psychobiological mechanisms involved in the stress response*

physiological reactivity — *quickening of the heart rate, blood pressure, and breathing resulting from exposure to internal or external cues that symbolize or resemble an aspect of the traumatic event*

play therapy — *a technique for treating young children in which they reveal their problems on a fantasy level with dolls, clay, and other toys*

post-synaptic neuron — *the downstream neuron that is the target of neurotransmission*

predictive validity — *the extent to which scores on an instrument predict actual performance*

pre-synaptic neuron — *the neuron that initiates neurotransmission by releasing the neurotransmitter into the synaptic cleft*

project — *the mechanism by which the client's intrapsychic processes infuse the therapeutic relationship*

psychic balance — *a dynamic equilibrium state between those thoughts, feelings, memories, and urges the conscious mind can tolerate and those it cannot*

psychic numbing — *is the inability to feel any emotions, either positive, such as love and pleasure, or negative, such as fear or guilt, also described as an "emotional anesthesia"*

psychodynamic approaches — *therapeutic approaches that focus on unconscious and conscious motivations and drives*

psychogenic amnesia — *the inability to remember emotionally charged events for psychological rather than neurological reasons*

psychological debriefing — *an intervention conducted by trained professionals shortly after a catastrophe, allowing victims to talk about their experience and receive information on "normal" types of reactions to such an event*

psychological probe — *a visual or auditory stimulus reminiscent of a traumatic experience to which a person with PTSD is exposed*

psychometric instruments — *tests which measure psychological factors such as personality, intelligence, beliefs, fears*

psychometric properties — *the elements of constructing a useful instrument such as establishing reliability and validity*

psychotic disorder — *mental disorder characterized by gross impairment in perceptions of reality*

R

receptors — *membrane bound protein molecules with a highly specific shape that facilitates binding by neurotransmitters or drugs*

reliability — *the extent to which the test produces similar results when administered at different times*

repression — *a hypothetical, unconscious process by which unacceptable (often trauma-related) thoughts and feelings are kept out of conscious awareness*

Rorschach Ink Blot Test — *a projective measure of personality assessment that utilizes "neutral" inkblots in which the client responds to the blot with their own experiences and perceptual orientation*

S

saccadic eye movements — *quick eye movements, jumping from one point of fixation to another*

secondary traumatization — *the feelings, personal distress, and symptoms that are sometimes evoked in people who live with an individual who has PTSD*

self-cohesion — *knowledge and integration of previously unconscious motivations*

sensitivity — *percent of cases correctly identified by the instrument*

somatization — *the expression of emotional distress through physical symptoms such as peptic ulcer, asthma, or chronic pain*

specificity — *percent of non-cases correctly identified by the instrument*

standardized — *data collected on a large group and results put in the form of averages by age and group*

Subjective Units of Distress Scale — *a scale ranging from 10-100 with 10 being the least anxiety provoking and 100 being the most anxiety provoking. The SUDS scoring system allows the client to express exactly how upsetting or distressing certain stimuli are in comparison to other anxiety experiences*

supportive PTSD treatments — *PTSD treatments that encourage skill building and problem solving for current issues in the client's life as an avenue for increasing adaptive functioning and regaining a sense of control*

sympathetic nervous system — *part of the autonomic nervous system that regulates arousal functions such as heart rate and blood flow*

synaptic cleft — *the space between one neuron and the next that must be traversed by neurotransmitters*

Symptom Checklist-90 (SCL-90) — *a broad-spectrum instrument that assesses many different psychological domains, including depressive, psychotic, and anxiety symptoms*

T

teratogenic — *producing fetal abnormalities during pregnancy*

test-retest reliability — *the extent to which those tested obtain similar scores each time they take the test*

trauma focus treatment — *PTSD treatments in which the client is directed to explore in depth the trauma as an avenue for healing*

V

validity — *the extent to which the instrument actually measures what it claims*

vicarious traumatization — *the feelings, personal distress, and symptoms that are sometimes evoked in clinicians who work with PTSD clients*

W

Wechsler Adult Intelligence Scale (WAIS) — *a widely used intelligence test designed to measure a person's intellectual potential and decision making processes*

well-encapsulated — *psychological buffers that prevent a person from experiencing a painful situation, such as refusing to read newspaper accounts of sexual abuse*

Bibliography

1. Kessler, R.C., Sonnega, A., Bromet, E., Hughes, M., & Nelson, C.B. (1995). Posttraumatic stress disorder in the National Comorbidity Survey. Archives of General Psychiatry, 52, 1048-1060.

2. American Psychiatric Committee on Nomenclature and Statistics (1980). Diagnostic and Statistical Manual of Mental Disorders (3rd ed.). Washington, DC: American Psychiatric Association.

3. American Psychiatric Committee on Nomenclature and Statistics (1994). Diagnostic and Statistical Manual of Mental Disorders (4th ed.). Washington, DC: American Psychiatric Association.

4. Shay, J. (1991). Learning about combat stress from Homer's Iliad. Journal of Traumatic Stress, 4, 561-579.

5. van der Kolk, B.A., Weisaeth, L. & van der Hart, O. (1996). History of trauma in psychiatry. In B.A. van der Kolk, A.C. McFarlane & L. Weisaeth (Eds.), Traumatic stress: The effects of overwhelming experience on mind, body, and society (pp. 47-74). New York/London; Guilford Press.

6. Trimble, M.R. (1985). Post-traumatic stress disorder: History of a concept. In C.R. Figley (Ed.), Trauma and its wake: Volume 1: The study and treatment of post-traumatic stress disorder (pp. 5-14). New York: Burnner/Mazel.

7. Cohen, M.E., White, P.D. & Johnson, R.E. (1948). Neurocirculatory asthenia, anxiety neurosis, or the effort syndrome. Archives of Internal Medicine, 81, 260-281.

8. Kardiner, A. (1941). The traumatic neurosis of war. New York: Hoeber.

9. Classen, C., Koopman, C., Hales, R. & Spiegel, D. (1998). Acute stress disorder as a predictor of post-traumatic stress symptoms. American Journal of Psychiatry, 155, 620-624.

10. Eriksson, N.G. & Lundin, T. (1996). Early traumatic stress reactions among Swedish survivors of the m/s Estonia disaster. British Journal of Psychiatry, 713-716.

11. Staab, J.P., Grieger, T.A., Fullerton, C.S. & Ursano, R.J. (1996). Acute stress disorder, subsequent posttraumatic stress disorder and depression after a series of typhoons. Anxiety, 2, 219-225.

12. Bryant, R.A. & Harvey, A.G. (1998). Relationship between acute stress disorder and posttraumatic stress disorder following mild traumatic brain injury. American Journal of Psychiatry, 155, 625-629.

13. Schnurr, P.P. (1991) PTSD and combat-related psychiatric symptoms in older veterans PTSD Research Quarterly, 2, 1-6.

14. Friedman, M.J., Rosenheck, R.A. (1996). PTSD as a persistent mental illness. In S. Soreff (Ed.), The seriously and persistently mentally ill: The state-of-the-art treatment handbook (pp.369-389). Seattle, WA: Hogrefe & Huber.

15. Harvey, A.G. & Bryant, R.A. (1998). Acute stress disorder after mild traumatic brain injury. Journal of Nervous & Mental Disorders, 186, 333-337.

16. Yehuda, R., & McFarlane, A.C. (1995). Conflict between current knowledge about posttraumatic stress disorder and its original conceptual basis. American Journal of Psychiatry, 152, 1705-1713.

17. Fairbank, J.A., Schlenger, W.E., Saigh, P.A. & Davidson, J.R.T. (1995). An epidemiologic profile of post-traumatic stress disorder: Prevalence, comorbidity, and risk factors. In M.J. Friedman, D.S. Charney & A.Y. Deutch (Eds.) Neurobiological and clinical consequences of stress: From normal adaptation to post-traumatic stress disorder, (pp. 415-427). Philadelphia, PA: Lippincott-Raven.

18. Wilson, J.P. & Keane, T.M. (1996). Assessing psychological trauma and PTSD. New York: Guilford.

19. Friedman, M.J. & Schnurr, P.P. (1995). The relationship between trauma and physical health. In M.J. Friedman, D.S. Charney, & A.Y. Deutch (Eds.), Neurobiological and clinical consequences of stress: From normal adaptation to post-traumatic stress disorder (pp. 507-526). Philadelphia: Lippincott-Raven.

20. Schnurr, P.P. & Jankowski, M.K. (in press). Physical health and posttraumatic stress disorder: Review and synthesis. Seminars in Clinical Neuropsychiatry.

21. Herman, J.L. (1992). Complex PTSD: A syndrome in survivors of prolonged and repeated trauma. Journal of Traumatic Stress, 5, 377-391.

22. Kofoed, L., Friedman, M.J. & Peck, R. (1993). Alcoholism and drug abuse in patients with PTSD. Psychiatric Quarterly, 64, 151-171.

23. Risse, S.C., Whitters, A., Burke, J., et al. (1990).Severe withdrawal symptoms after discontinuation of alprazolam in eight patients with combat induced post-traumatic stress disorder. Journal of Clinical Psychiatry, 51, 206-209.

24. Linehan, M.M., Tutek, D.A., Heard, H.L. & Armstrong, H.E. (1994). Interpersonal outcome of cognitive behavioral treatment for chronically suicidal borderline patients. American Journal of Psychiatry, 151, 1771-1776.

25. Marsella, A.J, Friedman, M.J., Gerrity, E.T. & Scurfield, R.M. (Eds.) (1996). Ethnocultural aspects of posttraumatic stress disorder: Issues research and clinical applications. Washington, DC: American Psychological Association.

26. Roth, S. & Friedman, M.J. (Eds.) (1998). Childhood trauma remembered: A report on the current scientific knowledge base and its applications. Northbrook, IL: International Society for Traumatic Stress Studies.

27. Williams, L.M. (1994). Recall of childhood trauma: A prospective study of women's memories of child sexual abuse. Journal of Consulting and Clinical Psychology, 62, 1167-1176.

28. Kinzie, D. (1989). Therapeutic approaches to traumatized Cambodian refugees. Journal of Traumatic Stress, 2, 75-91.

29. Gusman, F.D., Stewart, J., Young, B.H., Riney, S.J., Abueg, F.R. & Blake, D.D. (1996). A multicultural developmental approach for treating trauma. In A.J. Marsella, M.J. Friedman, E.T. Gerrity & R.M. Scurfield (Eds.), Ethnocultural aspects of posttraumatic stress disorder: Issues, research, and clinical applications (pp. 439-458). Washington, DC: American Psychological Association.

30. Stamm, B.H. & Friedman, M.J. (in press). Transcultural perspectives on post-traumatic stress disorder and other reactions to extreme stress. In A. Shalev, R. Yehuda & A. McFarlane (Eds.), Human response to trauma across cultural, gender, and life course. New York: Plenum Press.

31. Herman, J.L. & Schatzow, E. (1987). Recovery and verification of memories of childhood sexual trauma. Psychoanal Psychol, 4, 1-14.

32. Schacter, D.L. (1996). for memory. New York: Basic Books.

33. Lindsay, D.S., Read, J.D. (1994). Psychotherapy and memories of childhood sexual abuse: A cognitive perspective. Applied Cognitive Psychology, 8, 281-338.

34. Loftus, E.F. (1993). The reality of repressed memories. American Psychology, 48, 518-537.

35. Loftus, E.F., Polonsky, S. & Fullilove, M.T. (1994). Memories of childhood sexual abuse: Remembering and repressing. Psychology of Women Quarterly, 18, 67-84.

36. Schooler, J.W., Bendiksen, M. & Ambadar, Z. (1997). Taking the middle line: Can we accommodate both fabricated and recovered memories of sexual abuse? In I.M. Conway (Ed.), False and recovered memories (pp. 251-292). Oxford: Oxford University Press.

37. Pope, K.S. (1996). Memory, abuse, and science: Questioning claims about the false memory syndrome epidemic. American Psychologist, 51, 957-974.

38. Elliott, D.M. & Briere, J. (1995). Posttraumatic stress associated with delayed recall of sexual abuse: A general population study. Journal of Traumatic Stress, 8, 629-648.

39. Chu, J.A., Frey, L.M., Ganzel, B.L. & Mathews, J.A. (1999). Memories of childhood abuse: Dissociation, amnesia, and corroboration. American Journal of Psychiatry, 156, 749-755.

40. Herman, J. (1992). Trauma and recovery. New York: Basic Books.

41. Resick, P. Personal Communication. 10/24/99.

42. McCann, L. & Pearlman, A. (1990). Vicarious traumatization: A framework for understanding the psychological effects of working with victims. Journal of Traumatic Stress, 3, 131-149.

43. Figley, C.R. (1995). Compassion fatigue: Secondary traumatic stress disorders from treating the traumatized. New York: Brunner/Mazel.

44. Danieli, Y. (1984). Psychotherapists' participation in the conspiracy of silence about the Holocaust. Psychoanalytic Psychology, 1, 23-42.

45. Wilson, J. & Lindy, J. (1994). Countertransference in the treatment of PTSD. New York: Guilford Press.

46. Courtois, C.A. (1988). Healing the incest wound: Adult survivors in therapy. New York: W.W. Norton.

47. Gusman, F.D., Abueg, F.R. & Friedman, M.J. (1991). Operation Desert Storm Clinician Packet. Palo Alto, CA: National Center for PTSD.

48. Yassan, J. (1993). Group work with clinicians who have a history of trauma. NCP Clinical Newsletter, 3, 10-11.

49. Foa, E.B., Keane, T.M., & Friedman, M.J. (in press). Effective Treatments for PTSD: Practice Guidelines from the International Society for Traumatic Stress Studies. New York: Guilford.

50. Scurfield, R. (1993). Treatment of PTSD in Vietnam veterans. In J.P. Wilson & B. Raphael (Eds.), The international handbook of traumatic stress syndromes. New York: Plenum Press.

51. Lindy, J.D. (1993). Focal psychoanalytic psychotherapy. In J.P. Wilson & B. Raphael (Eds.). The international handbook of traumatic stress syndromes. New York: Plenum Press.

52. Horowitz, M.J. (1986). Stress response syndromes (2nd ed.). New York: Jason Aronson.

53. Foa, E.B. & Rothbaum, B.O. (1997). Treating the trauma of rape: A cognitive-behavioral therapy for PTSD. New York: Guilford.

54. Kardiner, A. & Spiegel, H. (1947). War stress and neurotic illness. New York: Paul B. Hoeber.

55. Solomon, Z. & Benbenishty, R. (1986). The role of proximity, immediacy, and expectancy in frontline treatment of combat stress reaction among Israelis in the Lebanon War. American Journal of Psychiatry, 143, 613-617.

56. Mitchell, J.T. (1983). When disaster strikes. Journal Of Emergency Medical Services, 8, 36-39.

57. Dyregrov, A. (1989). Caring for helpers in disaster situations: Psychological debriefing. Disaster Management, 2, 25-30.

58. Bisson, J.I., McFarlane, A.C. & Rose, S. (in press). Psychological debriefing. In E.B. Foa, T.M. Keane & M.J. Friedman (Eds.), Effective Treatments for PTSD: Practice Guidelines from the International Society for Traumatic Stress Studies. New York: Guilford.

59. Rothbaum, B.O., Meadows, E.A., Resick, P. & Foy, D.W. (in press). Cognitive-behavioral treatment. In E.B. Foa, T.M. Keane & M.J. Friedman (Eds.), Effective Treatments for PTSD: Practice Guidelines from the International Society for Traumatic Stress Studies. New York: Guilford.

60. Follette, V.M., Ruzek, J.I. & Abueg, F.R. (1998). Cognitive-behavioral therapies for trauma. New York: Guilford.

61. Foa, E.B. & Kozak, M.J. (1986). Emotional processing of fear: Exposure to corrective information. Psychological Bulletin, 99, 20-35.

62. Foa, E.B., Riggs, D.S., Massie, E.G. & Yarczower, M. (1995). The impact of fear activation and anger on the efficacy of exposure treatment for PTSD. Behavior Therapy, 26, 487-499.

63. Beck, A.T. (1976). Cognitive therapy and the emotional disorders. New York: International Universities Press.

64. Clark, D.M. (1986). A cognitive approach to panic. Behavior Research and Therapy, 24, 461-470.

65. Marks, I., Lovell, K., Noshirvani, H., Livanou, M. & Thrasher, S. (1998). Treatment of post-traumatic stress disorder by exposure and/or cognitive restructuring: A controlled study. Archives of General Psychiatry, 55, 317-325.

66. Brewin, C.R., Dalgleish, T. & Joseph, S. (1996). A dual representational theory of posttraumatic stress disorder. Psychological Review, 103, 670-686.

67. Tarrier, N., Pilgrim, H., Sommerfield, C., Faragher, B., Reynolds, M., Graham, E., & Barrowelough, C. (1999). A randomized trial of cognitive therapy and imaginal exposure in the treatment of chronic post-traumatic stress disorder. Journal of Consulting and Clincial Psychology, 67, 13-18.

68. Resick, P.A. & Schnicke, M.K. (1992). Cognitive processing therapy for sexual assault victims. Journal of Consulting and Clinical Psychology, 60, 748-756.

69. Resick, P.A. & Schnicke, M.K. (1993). Cognitive processing therapy for rape victims: A treatment manual. Newbury Park: SAGE Publications.

70. Resick, P.A., Nistith, P., & Astin, M. (1998, March). A controlled trial comparing cognitive processing therapy and prolonged exposure. Presented at Lake George Research Conference on Post-Traumatic Stress Disorder, Lake George, NY.

71. Wolpe, J. (1958). Psychotherapy for reciprocal inhibition. Stanford: Stanford University Press.

72. Wolpe, J. (1969). The practice of behavior therapy. Oxford: Pergamon Press.

73. Kilpatrick, D.G., Veronen, L.J. & Resick, P.A. (1982). Psychological sequelae to rape: Assessment and treatment strategies. In D.M. Dolays & R.L. Meredith (Eds.), Behavioral medicine: Assessment and treatment strategies (pp. 473-497). New York: Plenum.

74. Resick, P.A., Jordan, C.G., Girelli, S.A., Hutter, C.K. & Marhoefer-Dvorak, S. (1988). A comparative victim study of behavioral group therapy for sexual assault victims. Behavior Therapy, 19, 385-401.

75. Bryant, R.A., Sackville, T., Dang, S.T., Moulds, M., & Guthrie, R. (1999). Treating acute stress disorder: An evaluation of cognitive therapy and supportive counseling techniques. American Journal of Psychiatry, 156, 1780-1786.

76. Kudler, H., Blank, A. & Krupnick, J. (in press). The psychoanalytic psychotherapy of posttraumatic stress disorder. In E.B. Foa, T.M. Keane & M.J. Friedman (Eds.), Effective Treatments for PTSD: Practice Guidelines from the International Society for Traumatic Stress Studies. New York: Guilford.

77. Horowitz, M.J. (1974). Stress response syndromes: Character style and dynamic psychotherapy. Archives of General Psychiatry, 31, 768-781.

78. Krystal, H. (1988). Integration and self-healing. Hillsdale, NJ: The Analytic Press.

79. Lindy, J. (1996). Psychoanalytic psychotherapy of post-traumatic stress disorder. In B. van der Kolk, A. McFarlane & L. Weisaeth (Eds.), Traumatic Stress (pp. 525-536). New York: Guilford Press.

80. Brom, D., Kleber, R.J. & Defares, P.B. (1989). Brief psychotherapy for post-traumatic stress disorders. Journal of Consulting and Clinical Psychology, 57, 607-612.

81. Marmar, C. & Freeman, M. (1988). Brief dynamic psychotherapy for post-traumatic stress disorders: Management of narcissistic regression. Journal of Traumatic Stress, 1, 323-337.

82. Horowitz, M.J., Stinson, C., Curtis, D., Ewert, M., Redington, D., Singer, J.L., Bucci, W., Merganthaler, E., Milbrath, C. & Hartley, D. (1993). Topics and signs: Defensive control of emotional expression. Journal of Consulting and Clinical Psychology, 61, 421-430.

83. Horowitz, M.J., Milbrath, C., Jordan, D., Stinson, C., Ewert, M., Redington, D., Fridhandler, B., Reidbord, S. & Hartley, D. (1994). Expressive and defensive behavior during discourse on unresolved topics: A single case study. Journal of Personality, 62, 527-563.

84. Shapiro, F. (1989). Eye movement desensitization: A new treatment for post-traumatic stress disorder. Journal of Behavior Therapy and Experimental Psychiatry, 20, 211-217.

85. Shapiro, F. (1995). Eye movement desensitization and reprocessing: Basic principles, protocols, and procedures. New York: Guilford.

86. McNally, R.J. (1999). Research on eye movement desensitization and reprocessing (EMDR) as a treatment for PTSD. Research Quarterly, 10, 1-7.

87. Hyer, L. & Brandsma, J.M. (1997). EMDR minus eye movements equals good psychotherapy. Journal of Traumatic Stress, 10, 515-522.

88. Devilly, G.J. & Spence, S.H. (1999). The relative efficacy and treatment distress of EMDR and a cognitive behavioral trauma treatment protocol in the amelioration of post traumatic stress disorder. Journal of Anxiety Disorders, 13, 131-158.

89. Waysman, M., Mikulincer, M., Solomon, Z., et al. (1993). Secondary traumatization among wives of posttraumatic combat veterans: A family typology. Journal of Family Psychology, 7, 104-118.

90. Riggs, D.S. (in press). Marital and family therapy. In E.B. Foa, T.M. Keane & M.J. Friedman (Eds.), Effective Treatments for PTSD: Practice Guidelines from the International Society for Traumatic Stress Studies. New York: Guilford.

91. Figley, C.R. (1989). Helping traumatized families. San Francisco: Jossey-Bass.

92. Johnson, D.R., Feldman, S.C. & Lubin, H. (1995). Critical interaction therapy: Couples therapy in combat-related posttraumatic stress disorder. Family Process, 34, 401-412.

93. Harris, C.J. (1991). A family crisis-intervention model for the treatment of post-traumatic stress reaction. Journal of Traumatic Stress, 4, 195-207.

94. Rosenheck, R. & Thompson, J. (1986). "Detoxification" of Vietnam war trauma: A combined family-individual approach. Family Process, 25, 559-570.

95. Williams, C.M. & Williams, T. (1980). Family therapy for Vietnam veterans. In T. Williams (Ed.), Post-traumatic stress disorder of the Vietnam veteran. Cincinnati, OH: Disabled American Veterans.

96. Mio, J.S. & Foster, J.D. (1991). The effects of rape upon victims and families: Implications for a comprehensive family therapy. The American Journal of Family Therapy, 19(2), 147-159.

97. Foy, D.W., Glynn, S.M., Schnurr, P.P., Weiss, D.S., Wattenberg, M.S., Marmar, C.R., Kankowski, M.K. & Gusman, F.D. (In press). Group psychotherapy for posttraumatic stress disorder. In E.B. Foa, T.M. Keane & M.J. Friedman (Eds.), Effective Treatments for PTSD: Practice Guidelines from the International Society for Traumatic Stress Studies. New York: Guilford.

98. Yalom, I.D. (1975). The theory and practice of group psychotherapy. New York: Basic Books.

99. Foy, D.W., Ruzek, J.I., Glynn, S.M., Riney, S.A. & Gusman, F.D. (1997). Trauma focus group therapy for combat-related PTSD. In Session: Psychotherapy in Practice, 3, 59-73.

100. Lubin, H., Loris, M., Burt, J. & Johnson, D.R. (1998). Efficacy of psychoeducational group therapy in reducing symptoms of posttraumatic stress disorder among multiply traumatized women. American Journal of Psychiatry, 155, 1172-1177.

101. Penk, W., Binus, G., Herz, L., et al. (in press). Psychosocial rehabilitation techniques. In E.B. Foa, T.M. Keane & M.J. Friedman (Eds.), Effective Treatments for PTSD: Practice Guidelines from the International Society for Traumatic Stress Studies. New York: Guilford.

102. Bell, M.D., Lysaker, P.H. & Milstein, R.M. (1996). Clinical benefits of paid work activity in schizophrenia. Schizophrenia Bulletin, 22, 51-67.

103. Drake, R.E. (1996). The New Hampshire study of supported employment for people with severe mental illness. Consulting and Clinical Psychology, 64, 390-398.

104. Drake, R.E., McHugo, G.J., Becker, D.R. & Anthony, W.A. (1996). The New Hampshire study of supported employment for people with severe mental illness. Consulting and Clinical Psychology, 64, 391-399.

105. Pynoos, R.S. (1993). Traumatic stress and developmental psychopathology in children and adolescents. In J.M. Oldham, M.B. Riba & A. Tasman (Eds.), Review of Psychiatry, Volume 12 (pp. 205-238), Washington, DC: American Psychiatric Press, Inc.

106. Pynoos, R.S., Steinberg, A.M. & Wraith, R. (1995). A developmental model of childhood traumatic stress. In D. Cicchetti & D. Cohen (Eds.), Manual of developmental psychology, vol 2: Risk, disorder, and adaptation. New York: John Wiley.

107. Terr, L.C. (1989). Treating psychic trauma in children. Journal of Traumatic Stress, 2, 3-19.

108. Putnam, F.W. (1997). Dissociation in children and adolescents: A developmental perspective. New York: Guilford.

109. Herman, J.L., Perry, J.C., van der Kolk, B.A. (1989). Childhood trauma in borderline personality disorder. American Journal of Psychiatry, 146, 490-495.

110. Lyons, J.A. (1987). Posttraumatic stress disorder in children and adolescents: A review of the literature. Journal of Developmental Behavior Pediatrics, 8, 349-356.

111. Cohen, J.A., Berliner, L. & March, J.S. (in press). PTSD treatment guidelines for children and adolescents. In E.B. Foa, T.M. Keane & M.J. Friedman (Eds.), Effective Treatments for PTSD: Practice Guidelines from the International Society for Traumatic Stress Studies. New York: Guilford.

112. Goenjian, A.K., Pynoos, R.S., Steinberg, A.M., et al. (1995). Psychiatric comorbidity in children after the 1988 earthquake in Armenia. Journal of the American Academy of Child & Adolescent Psychiatry, 34, 1174-1184.

113. March, J.L., Amaya-Jackson, L., et al. (1998). Cognitive-behavioral psychotherapy for children and adolescents with post-traumatic stress disorder following a single incident stressor. Journal of the American Academy of Child and Adolescent Psychiatry, 37, 585-593.

114. Pynoos, R.S. & Nader, K. (1988). Psychological first aid and treatment approach to children exposed to community violence: Research implications. Journal of Traumatic Stress, 1, 445-473.

115. Chemtob, C.M., Tomas, S., Law, W., Cremniter, D. (1997). Post-disaster psychosocial intervention: A field study of the impact of debriefing on psychological distress. American Journal of Psychiatry, 154, 415-417.

116. Berliner, L. & Saunders, B.E. (1996). Treating fears and anxiety in sexually abused children: Results of a controlled two year study. Journal of Maltreatment, I, 294-309.

117. Cannon, W.B. (1932). The Wisdom of the body. New York: Norton.

118. Selye, H. The general adaptation syndrome and the diseases of adaptation. Journal of Clinical Endocrinol, 6, 117-230.

119. Southwick, S.M., Paige, S.R., Morgan, C.A., Bremner, J.D., Krystal, J.H. & Charney, D.S. (1999). Adrenergic and serotonergic abnormalities in PTSD: Catecholamines and serotonin. Seminars in Clinical Neuropsychiatry.

120. Chrousos, G.P. & Gold, P.W. (1992). The concepts of stress and stress system disorders: Overview of physical and behavioral homeostasis. JAMA, 267, 1244-1252.

121. Friedman, M.J., Charney, D.S., Deutch, A.Y. (Eds.) (1995). Neurobiological and Clinical Consequences of Stress: From Normal Adaptation to PTSD. Philadelphia, PA: Lippincott-Raven Press.

122. Yehuda, R., & McFarlane, A.C. (1997). Psychobiology of Posttraumatic Stress Disorder. Annals of the New York Academy of Sciences, 821.

123. Friedman, M.J. (Ed.), (1999). Progress in the research on the psychobiology of PTSD. Seminars in Clinical Neuropsychiatry, 4, 229-316.

124. Bremner, J.D. (1999). Alterations in brain structure and function associated with posttraumatic stress disorder. Seminars in Clinical Neuropsychiatry, 4, 249-255.

125. Debellis, M.D., Keshavan, M.S., Clark D.B., Casey, B.J., Giedd, J.N., Boring, A.M., Frustaci, K., and Ryan, N.D. (1999). Developmental traumatology Part II: Brain development. Biological Psychiatry, 45,1271-1284.

126. DeBellis, M.D., Baum, A.S., Birmahr, B., Keshavan, M.S., Eccard, C.H., Boring, A.M., Jenkins, F.J., and Ryan, N.D. (1999). Developmental traumatology Part I: Biological stress systems. Biological Psychiatry, 45,1259-1270.

127. Malloy, P., Fairbank, J. & Keane, T. Validation of a multimethod assessment of posttraumatic stress disorder in Vietnam veterans. Journal of Consulting and Clinical Psychology, 51, 488-493.

128. Pitman, R., Orr, S., Forgue, D., et al. (1987). Psychophysiologic assessment of posttraumatic stress disorder imagery in Vietnam combat veterans. Archives of General Psychiatry, 44, 970-975.

129. Southwick, S.M., Krystal, J.H., Morgan, A.C., et al.(1993). Abnormal noradrenergic function in post-traumatic stress disorder. Archives of General Psychiatry, 50, 266-274.

130. Yehuda, R., Boisoneau, D., Mason, J.W., Giller, E.L. (1993). Relationship between lymphocyte gluco-corticoid receptor number and urinary-free cortisol excretion in mood, anxiety and psychotic disorders. Biological Psychiatry, 34,18-25.

131. Mason, J.W., Giller, E.L., Kosten, T.R., et al. (1986). Urinary-free cortisol levels in post-traumatic stress disorder patients. Journal of Nervous & Mental Disease, 174, 145-159.

132. Yehuda, R., Southwick, S.M., Krystal, J.H. (1993). Enhanced suppression of cortisol following a low dose of dexamethasone in combat veterans with posttraumatic stress disorder. American Journal of Psychiatry, 150, 83-86.

133. Bremner, J.D., Licinio, J., Darnell, A., et al. (1997). Elevated CSF corticotropin-releasing factor concentrations in post-traumatic stress disorder. American Journal of Psychiatry, 154, 624-629.

134. Friedman, M.J., Davidson, J.R.T., Mellman, T.A. & Southwick, S.M. Practice Guideline for Pharmaco-therapy for PTSD. E. Foa, T. Keane & M.J. Friedman (Eds.), Effective Treatments for PTSD: Practice Guidelines from the International Society for Traumatic Stress Studies. New York: Guilford Press.

135. Brady, K.T., Sonne, S.C. & Roberts, J.M. (1995). Sertraline treatment of comorbid posttraumatic stress disorder and alcohol dependence. Journal of Clinical Psychiatry, 56, 502-505.

136. Friedman, M.J. (1990). Interrelationships between biological mechanisms and pharmacotherapy of post-traumatic stress disorder. In M.E. Wolfe & A.D. Mosnaim (Eds.), Post-Traumatic Stress Disorder: Etiology, Phenomenology, and Treatment (pp. 204-225). Washington, DC: American Psychiatric Press.

137. Hertzberg, M.A., Feldman, M.E., Beckham, J.C., et al. (1996). Trial of trazadone for posttraumatic stress disorder using a multiple baseline group design. Journal of Clinical Psychopharmacology, 16, 294-298.

138. Hertzberg, M.A., Feldman, M.E., Beckham, J.C., et al. (1998). Open trial of nefazodone for combat-related posttraumatic stress disorder. Journal of Clinical Psychiatry. 59, 00-00.

139. DeMartino, R., Mollica, R.F. & Wilk, V. (1995). Monoamine oxidase inhibitors in posttraumatic stress disorder. Journal of Nervous Mental Disorders, 183, 510-515.

140. Southwick, S.M., Yehuda, R., Giller, El, et al. (1994). Use of tricyclics and monoamine oxidase inhibitors in the treatment of PTSD: A quantitative review. M.M. Murburg (Ed.), Catecholamine function in post-traumatic stress disorder: Emerging concepts (pp. 293-305). Washington, DC: American Psychiatry Press.

141. Friedman, M.J. & Southwick, S.M. (1995). Towards pharmacotherapy for PTSD. M.J. Friedman, D.S. Charney & A.Y. Deutch (Eds.), Neurobiological and Clinical Consequences of Stress: From Normal Adaptation to PTSD (pp. 465-481). Philadelphia, PA: Lippincott-Raven Press.

142. Braun, P., Greenberg, D., Dasberg, H., et al. (1990). Core symptoms of posttraumatic stress disorder unimproved by alprazolam treatment. Journal of Clinical Psychiatry, 51, 236-238.

143. Post, R.M., Weiss, S.R.B. & Smith, M. A. (1995). Sensitization and kindling: Implications for the evolving neural substrate of PTSD. In M.J. Friedman, D.S. Charney, A.Y. Deutch (Eds.), Neurobiological and Clinical Consequences of Stress: From Normal Adaptation to PTSD (pp. 203-224). Philadelphia, PA: Lippincott-Raven Press.

144. Norris, F. (1990). Screening for traumatic stress: A scale for use in the general population. Journal of Applied Social Psychology, 20, 1704-1718.

145. Kilpatrick, D., Resnick, H. & Freedy, J. (1991, unpublished instrument). The Potential Stressful Events Interview. Charleston, South Carolina: Medical University of South Carolina.

146. Vrana, S. & Lauterbach, D. (1994). Prevalence of traumatic events and post-traumatic psychological symptoms in a nonclinical sample of college students. Journal of Traumatic Stress, 7, 289-302.

147. Krinsley, K.E. & Weathers, F.W. (1995). The assessment of trauma in adults. PTSD Research Quarterly, 6, 1-6.

148. Sanders, B. & Becker-Lausen, E. (1995). The measurement of psychological maltreatment: Early data on the Child Abuse and Trauma Scale. Child Abuse & Neglect, 19, 315-323.

149. Bernstein, D.P., Fink, L., Handelsman, L., et al. (1994). Initial reliability and validity of a new retrospective measure of child abuse and neglect. American Journal of Psychiatry, 151, 1132-1136.

150. Ogata, S.N., Silk, K.R., Goodrich, S., Lohr, N.E., Westen, D. & Hill, E.M. (1990). Childhood sexual and physical abuse in adult patients with borderline personality disorder. American Journal of Psychiatry, 147, 1008-1013.

151. Gallagher, R.E., Flye, B.L., Hurt, S.W., Stone, M.H. & Hull, J.W. (1992). Retrospective assessment of traumatic experiences (RATE). Journal of Personality Disorders, 6, 99-108.

152. Bremner, J.D., Randall, P., Scott, T.M., Capelli, S., Delany, R., McCarthy, G. & Charney, D.S. (1995). Deficits in short-term memory in adult survivors of childhood abuse. Psychiatry Research, 59, 97-107.

153. Straus, M. (1979). Measuring intrafamily conflict and violence: The Conflict Tactics (CT) Scales. Journal of Marriage and the Family, 41, 75-88.

154. Shepard, M.F. & Campbell, J.A. (1992). The Abusive Behavior Inventory: A measure of psychological and physical abuse. Journal of Interpersonal Violence, 7, 291-305.

155. Koss, M.P. & Gidycz, C.A. (1985). Sexual experiences survey: Reliability and validity. Journal of Consulting and Clinical Psychology, 53, 422-423.

156. Wyatt, G.E., Lawrence, J., Vodounon, A. & Mickey, M.R. (1992). The Wyatt Sex History Questionnaire: A structured interview for female sexual history taking. Journal of Child Sexual Abuse, 1(4), 51-68.

157. Keane, T.M., Fairbank, J.A., Caddell, J.M., Zimering, R.T., Taylor, K.L. & Mora, C.A. (1989). Clinical evaluation of a measure to assess combat exposure. Psychological Assessment, 1, 53-55.

158. Wolfe, J., Brown, P.J., Furey, J. & Levin, K.B. (1993). Development of a wartime stressor scale for women. Psychological Assessment, 5, 330-335.

159. Mollica, R.F., Caspi-Yavin, Y., Bollini, P., Truong, T., Tor, S. & Lavelle, J. (1992). The Harvard Trauma Questionnaire: Validating a cross-cultural instrument for measuring torture, trauma, and posttraumatic stress disorder in Indochinese refugees. Journal of Nervous and Mental Disease, 180, 111-116.

160. First, M.B., Spitzer, R.L., Williams, J.B.W. & Gibbon, M. (1996). Structured Clinical Interview for DSM-IV. New York: New York State Psychiatric Institute, Biometrics Research.

161. Blake, D.D., Weathers, F.W., Nagy, L.M., Kaloupek, D.G., Gusman, F.D., Charney, D.S. & Keane, T.M. (1995). The development of a clinician-administered PTSD scale. Journal of Traumatic Stress, 8, 75-90.

162. Watson, C., Juba, M., Manifold, V., Kucala, T. & Anderson, P. (1991). The PTSD Interview: Rationale, description, reliability and concurrent validity of a DSM-III based technique. Journal of Clinical Psychology, 47, 179-185.

163. Davidson, J.R.T., Book, S.W., Colket, J.T., Tupler, L.A., Roth, S., David, D., Hertzberg, M., Mellman, T., Beckham, J.C., Smith, R.D., Davidson, R.M., Katz, R. & Feldman, M.E. (1997). Assessment of a new self-rating scale for posttraumatic stress disorder. Psychological Medicine, 27, 153-160.

164. World Health Organization (1997). Composite International Diagnostic Interview (CIDI), Version 2.1. Geneva: World Health Organization.

165. Robins, L.N., Cottler, L., Bucholz, K. (1995). Diagnostic Interview Schedule for DSM-IV. St. Louis: Washington University.

166. Breslau, N., Kessler, R., Peterson, E.L., (1998). PTSD assessment with a structured interview: Reliability and concordance with a standard clinical interview. International Journal of Methods & Psychiatric Research, 7, 121-127.

167. Weathers, F.W., Litz, B.T., Herman, D.S., Huska, J.A. & Keane, T.M. (1995). PTSD Checklist (PCL). Boston: National Center for PTSD.

168. Foa, E., Riggs, D., Dancu, C. & Rothbaum, B. (1993). Reliability and validity of a brief instrument for assessing post-traumatic stress disorder. Journal of Traumatic Stress, 6, 459-474.

169. Lyons, J. & Keane, T. (1992). Keane PTSD Scale: MMPI and MMPI-2 update. Journal of Traumatic Stress, 5, 111-117.

170. Schlenger, W. & Kulka, R.A. (1989). PTSD scale development for the MMPI-2. Research Triangle Park, NC: Research Triangle Park Institute.

171. Saunders, B., Arata, C. & Kilpatrick, D. (1990). Development of a crime-related posttraumatic stress disorder scale for women with the Symptom Checklist-90 Revised. Journal of Traumatic Stress, 3, 439-448.

172. Weiss, D.S. & Marmar, C.R. (1997). The Impact of Event Scale—Revised. In J.P. Wilson & T.M. Keane (Eds.), Assessing psychological trauma and PTSD (pp. 399-411). London: Guilford Press.

173. Keane, T.M., Caddell, J.M. & Taylor, K.L. (1988). Mississippi Scale for Combat-Related Posttraumatic Stress Disorder: Three studies in reliability and validity. Journal of Consulting and Clinical Psychology, 56, 85-90.

174. Norris, F. & Perilla, J. (1996). Reliability, validity, and cross-language stability of the Revised Civilian Mississippi Scale for PTSD. Journal of Traumatic Stress, 9, 285-298.

175. Hammarberg, M. (1992). Penn Inventory for Posttraumatic Stress Disorder: Psychometric properties. Psychological Assessment, 4, 67-76.

176. Briere, J. & Runtz, M. (1989). The Trauma Symptom Checklist (TSC-33): Early data on a new scale. Journal of Interpersonal Violence, 4, 151-163.

177. Briere, J. (1995). Trauma Symptom Inventory (TSI): Professional manual. Odessa, FL: Psychological Assessment Resources.

178. Freinkel, A. & Koopman, S.D. (1994). Dissociative symptoms in media eyewitnesses of an execution. American Journal of Psychiatry, 151, 1335-1339.

179. Marmar, C.R., Weiss, D.S. & Metzler, T.J. (1997). The Peritraumatic Dissociative Experiences Questionnaire. In In J.P. Wilson & T.M. Keane (Eds.), Assessing psychological trauma and PTSD (pp. 412-447). London: Guilford Press.

180. Nader, K.O. (1997). Assessing Traumatic Experiences in Children. In J.P. Wilson & T.M. Keane (Eds.), Assessing psychological trauma and PTSD (pp. 291-348). London: Guilford Press.

181. National Center for Study of Corporal Punishment and Alternatives in Schools. (1992). My Worst Experience Survey. Philadelphia, PA: Temple University Press.

182. Stamm, B.H. (Ed.) (1996). Measurement of stress, trauma and adaptation (pp. 386-387). Lutherville, MD: Sidran Press.

183. Fletcher, K. (1991). When Bad Things Happen Scale. (Available from the author, University of Massachusetts Medical Center, Dept. of Psychiatry, 55 Lake Avenue North, Worcester, MA 01655.)

184. Friedrich, W. (1995). Evaluation and treatment: The clinical use of the Child Sexual Behavior Inventory: Commonly asked questions. American Professional Society on the Abuse of Children (APSAC) Advisor, 8(1), 17-20.

185. Praver, F. (1994). Child Rating Scales - Exposure to Interpersonal Abuse. Unpublished copyrighted instrument.

186. Praver, F., Pelcovitz, D. & DiGiuseppe, R. (1994). The Angie/Andy Child Rating Scales, (Available from Praver, 5 Marseilles Drive, Locust Valley, NY 11560; Pelcovitz, Dept. of Psychiatry, 400 Community Drive, Manhasset, NY 11030; or DiGiuseppe, Psychology Dept. St. John's University, Grand Central and Utopia Parkways, Jamaica, NY 11439.)

187. Selner-O'Hasan, M.B., Kindlon, D.J., Buka, S.L., Raudenbush, S.W., & Earls, F.J. (1998). Assessing exposure to violence in urban youth. Journal of Child Psychology/Psychiatry, 39, 215-224.

188. Reich, W., Shayka, J.J. & Taibleson, C. (1991). Diagnostic Interview for Children and Adolescents (DICA). St. Louis, MO: Washington University.

189. Nader, K.O., Kriegler, J.A., Blake, D.D. & Pynoos, R.S. (1994b). Clinician Administered PTSD Scale, Child and Adolescent Version (CAPS-C). White River Junction, VT: National Center for PTSD.

190. Shaffer, D., Fisher, P., Dulcan, M., Davies, M., Piacentini, J., Schwab-Stone, M., Lahey, B.B., Bourdon, K., Jensen, P., Bird, H., Canino, G. & Regier, D. (in press). The NIMH Diagnostic Interview Schedule for Children (DISC-2.3): Description, acceptability, prevalences, and performance in the MECA study. Journal of the American Academy of Child and Adolescent Psychiatry.

191. Frederick, C., Pynoos, R. & Nader, K. (1992). Childhood PTSD Reaction Index (CPTS-RI). (Available from Frederick and Pynoos, 760 Westwood Plaza, Los Angeles, CA 90024; or Nader, P.O. Box 2251, Laguna Hills, CA 92654.)

192. Jones, R.T. (1994). Child's Reaction to Traumatic Events Scale (CRTES): A self report traumatic stress measure. (Available from the author, Dept. of Psychology, Stress and Coping Lab, 4102 Derring Hall, Virginia Polytechnic Institute and State University, Blacksburg, VA 24060).

193. Wolfe, V.V., Wolfe, D.A., Gentile, C. & Larose, L. (1986). Children's Impact of Traumatic Events Scale (CITES). (Available from Wolfe, Dept. of Psychology, London Health Sciences Center, 800 Commissioners Road East, London, Ontario (N6A4G5).

194. Briere, J. (1996a). Trauma Symptom Checklist for Children (TSCC). Odessa, FL: Psychological Assessment Resources.

195. Briere, J. (1996b). Trauma Symptom Checklist for Children (TSCC) professional manual. Odessa, FL: Psychological Assessment Resources.

196. Putnam, F.W. (1988). Child Dissociative Checklist. (Available from the author at National Institute of Mental Health, Building 15K, 9000 Rockville Pike, Bethesda, MD 20892-2668).

A

Abusive Behavior Inventory (ABI) 23, 81
acute 3, 8, 13, 17-18, 30, 39, 40
Acute Stress Disorder 3, 17-18, 20, 39, 41, 51, 86
Acute Stress Reaction Questionnaire (ASRQ) 86
adrenergic response 66-68, 75, 91
adrenocorticotropic hormone (ACTH) 67
age 21, 61
Alcohol Abuse/Dependence 24-25, 29-30, 77-78
Alprazolam 73, 76, 91
Amitriptyline 72
amygdala 66-67
Angie/Andy CRS (A/A CRS) 23, 88
anti-adrenergic agents 71-72, 75
    Clonidine 72, 75-78
    Propranolol 72, 75-78
antianxiety agents 71, 73, 76
    Alprazolam 73, 76, 91
    Clonazepam 73, 76, 91
anticonvulsants 71, 73, 76
    Carbamazepine 73
    Valproate 73, 76
antipsychotics 71, 73, 76-78
    Clozapine 73
    Risperidone 73, 77
    Thioridazine 73
ASD 3, 86
    similarities and differences between PTSD & ASD 10,17
Assertiveness Training 46, 50-52, 59
assessment 5, 7, 18-19, 22-23, 26, 31, 42, 79, 81-83, 85, 87-89
    Abusive Behavior Inventory (ABI) 23, 81
    Acute Stress Reaction Questionnaire (ASRQ) 86
    Angie/Andy CRS (A/A CRS) 23, 88
    Child Abuse and Trauma Scale 23, 80
    Child Dissociative Checklist (CDC) 23, 90
    Child Post-Traumatic Stress Reaction Index (CPTS-R) 23, 89
    Child Rating Scales of Exposure to Interpersonal A 23, 88
    Childhood Trauma Questionnaire 23, 80
    Children's Impact of Traumatic Events Scale (CITES) 23, 90
    Children's Sexual Behavior Inventory 3 (CSBI-3) 23, 88
    Child's Reaction to Traumatic Events Scale (CRTES) 23, 90
    Civilian Mississippi Scale 23, 85
    Clinician Administered PTSD Scale (CAPS) 23, 83
    Clinician Administered PTSD Scale for Children (CAPS-C) 89
    Combat Exposure Scale (CES) 23, 82
    Composite International Diagnostic Interview (CIDI) 23, 83
    Conflict Tactics Scale (CTS) 23, 81
    diagnostic instruments 20, 82-84, 87, 89
    Diagnostic Interview for Children and Adolescents

(DICA) 23, 89
Diagnostic Interview Schedule for Children (DISC) 23, 89
Diagnostic Interview Schedule - IV (DIS-IV) 23, 84
Early Trauma Inventory (ETI) 23, 81
Evaluation of Lifetime Stressors (ELS) 23, 80
Familial Experiences Inventory 23, 80
Harvard Trauma Questionnaire (HTQ) 23, 82
Impact of Event Scale – Revised (IES-R) 23, 85
instruments 23, 79-90
Mississippi Scale for Combat-Related PTSD (M-PTSD) 23, 85
My Exposure to Violence (My-ETV) 23, 88
My Worst Experience Survey (MWES) 23, 87
My Worst School Experience Survey (MWSES) 23, 87
Penn Inventory 23, 85
Peritraumatic Dissociative Experiences Questionnaire 86
PK-Scale of the MMPI-2 23, 84
Potential Stressor Experiences Inventory (PSEI) 23, 79
PS-Scale of the MMPI-2 23, 84
PTSD Checklist (PCL) 23, 84
PTSD Symptom Scale (PSS) 23, 84
PTSD-Interview 23, 83
Retrospective Assessment of Traumatic Experiences 23, 81
SCL-PTSD 23
Sexual Experiences Survey (SES) 23, 81
Structured Clinical Interview for DSM-IV (SCID) 23, 82
Symptom Checklist- PTSD (SCL-PTSD) 23, 85
Symptom Severity Scales 22, 86
The Davidson Self-Rating PTSD Scale 23, 83
Trauma Exposure Scales 20, 79-82, 87-88
Trauma Symptom Checklist-40 (TSC-40) 23, 85
Trauma Symptom Checklist for Children (TSCC) 23, 90
Trauma Symptom Inventory (TSI) 23, 85
Traumatic Event Screening Instrument (TESI) 23, 87
Traumatic Events Questionnaire (TEQ) 23, 80
Traumatic Stress Schedule (TSS) 23
When Bad Things Happen Scale (WBTHS) 23, 87
Women's Wartime Stressor Scale (WWSS) 23, 82
Wyatt Sex History Questionnaire (WSHQ) 23, 81
Attention Deficit Hyperactivity Disorder 21
avoidance 3-4, 12, 16, 19, 26, 36, 51, 54-55, 59, 62, 83, 86, 90

B

Biofeedback and Relaxation Training 46, 49, 52
Borderline Personality Disorder 61, 91

C

CAPS. *See* Clinician Administered PTSD Scale
Carbamazepine 73
catastrophic event 2, 10, 20, 25, 39, 48
CBT. *See* Cognitive Behavioral Therapy

cerebral cortex 66-67

characteristics 7-8

Child Abuse and Trauma Scale 23, 80

Child Dissociative Checklist (CDC) 23, 90

Child Post-Traumatic Stress Reaction Index (CPTS-R) 23, 89

Child Rating Scales of Exposure to Interpersonal Abuse (CRS-EIA) 23, 88

childhood trauma 21, 23, 28, 33-35, 44, 61-62, 80

Childhood Trauma Questionnaire 23, 80

children and adolescents 27, 33-35, 44, 61-62, 87-90
    Art and Play Therapy 62
    Cognitive Behavioral Therapy 61, 91
    Psychoeducational 63
    Psychological Debriefing 62
    Stress Inoculation Training (SIT) 62

Children's Impact of Traumatic Events Scale (CITES) 23, 90

Children's Sexual Behavior Inventory 3 (CSBI-3) 23, 88

Child's Reaction to Traumatic Events Scale (CRTES) 23, 90

chronic 1, 4, 13, 17, 19, 26, 28, 39, 59, 60, 75, 88

CISD. *See* Critical Incident Stress Debriefing

Civilian Mississippi Scale 23, 85

clinical interview 18, 19, 21-23

Clinician Administered PTSD Scale (CAPS) 23, 82-83

Clinician Administered PTSD Scale for Children (CAPS-C) 89

Clonazepam 73, 76, 91

Clonidine 72, 75-78

Clozapine 73

Cognitive Processing Therapy (CPT) 45, 48-50, 52, 55, 59

Cognitive Therapy 45, 47-48, 51-52, 54-55, 56, 58, 63

Cognitive Behavioral Therapy (CBT) 44-45, 49-52, 55-59, 61-63, 78
    Assertiveness Training 46, 50-52, 59
    Biofeedback and Relaxation Training 46, 49, 52
    Cognitive Processing Therapy 45, 48-52, 55, 59
    Cognitive Therapy 45-48, 51-52, 54-55, 56, 58, 63
    Exposure Therapy 33, 45-48, 51-52, 55
    Stress Inoculation Training (SIT) 45, 52
    Systematic Desensitization 46, 52

Combat Exposure Scale (CES) 23, 82

combined treatment 31-32

comorbid disorder 23-24, 29-32, 77-78, 91
    Alcohol Abuse/Dependence 24
    Conduct Disorder 24
    Drug Abuse/Dependence 24
    Dysthymia 24
    Generalized Anxiety Disorder 24
    Major Depressive Disorder 24
    Panic Disorder 24
    Simple Phobia 24
    Social Phobia 24

Complex PTSD 26, 31-32, 88

Composite International Diagnostic Interview (CIDI) 23, 83

Conduct Disorder 24

Conflict Tactics Scale (CTS) 23, 81

Corticotropin Releasing Factor (CRF) 66, 69

cortisol 67, 91

countertransference 35-36, 91

CPT. *See* Cognitive Processing Therapy

criteria 1-5,7, 10, 12-13, 17-19, 21, 23-26, 32-36, 52, 55-56, 62, 83

Critical Incident Stress Debriefing (CISD) 39-40

cross-cultural considerations 31, 33

D

delayed onset 5, 13

depersonalization 18, 86, 91

depression 4, 20, 24, 30, 32, 72-73, 77, 90

derealization 18, 86, 91

Desipramine 70-72, 75, 78

dexamethasone suppression test, DST 69, 91

diagnose 3, 7, 10, 17, 22, 26

Diagnostic and Statistical Manual of Mental Disorders 1-3, 12-13

diagnostic criteria 1-5, 7, 10, 12, 18-19, 21, 23, 25, 32-33, 52, 55, 62

diagnostic instruments 7, 21-22, 79, 82-83, 87, 89

Diagnostic Interview for Children and Adolescents 23, 89

Diagnostic Interview Schedule for Children (DISC) 23, 89

Diagnostic Interview Schedule IV (DIS-IV) 23, 84

DISC. *See* Diagnostic Interview Schedule for Children

dissociation 3-4, 21, 25-26, 32, 61, 90, 91

dissociative amnesia 17, 90, 91

Dissociative Identity Disorder 26, 61, 91

dissociative symptoms 4, 17-18, 33, 41, 63, 77, 86, 90

drug abuse/dependence 24-25, 29-30, 77-78

DSM-III 1-3

DSM-IV 2-3, 7, 9-13, 17, 21, 23-24, 32-33, 82-83, 88

Dysthymia 24

E

Early Trauma Inventory (ETI) 23, 81

education 4, 21, 40, 42, 57, 60

EMDR. *See* Eye Movement Desensitization and Reprocessing

Evaluation of Lifetime Stressors (ELS) 23, 80

Exposure Therapy 32, 45-48, 50-52, 55

Eye Movement Desensitization and Reprocessing (EMDR) 44, 54-56

F

Familial Experiences Inventory 23, 80

Fight or Flight Reaction 66

flashback 9, 12, 68, 86

Fluoxetine 70-74, 77

Fluvoxamine 70-74, 77

G

gender 20, 21, 88

General Adaptation Syndrome 65, 66

Generalized Anxiety Disorder 24, 92

genetic 21

global treatment issues 27

Group Therapy 33, 57, 58, 59
    Cognitive Behavioral Focus Group Therapy 58
    Psychodynamic Focus Group Therapy 58

Supportive Group Therapy 59

H

hallucination 8, 90, 92
Harvard Trauma Questionnaire (HTQ) 23, 82
hippocampus 66-68
HPA system 67, 69
Human Stress Response 65, 67, 69-70
    Fight or Flight Reaction 66
    General Adaptation Syndrome 66
hyperarousal 3-4, 7-9, 13, 16, 24-25, 28, 30, 36,
    45, 47, 53, 55, 71, 73-74, 77-78, 90
hypervigilant 17, 19, 77
hypothalamic-pituitary-adrenocortical (HPA) axis 66, 92
hypothalamus 66, 67

I

Imipramine 70-72, 75, 78
Impact of Event Scale–Revised (IES-R) 23, 85
individual psychotherapy 44
    Cognitive-Behavioral Therapy (CBT) 44-45, 49-52, 55-
        59, 61-63, 78
    Eye Movement Desensitization and Reprocessing
        (EMDR) 44, 54-56
    Psychodynamic Psychotherapy 44, 53-54
instruments 5, 7, 18-23, 79-85, 90 (also see assessment)
interviews 19, 80
intrusive recollections 8, 14-17, 26, 28, 36, 38, 73-75

L

lifetime PTSD 4, 23

M

Major Depressive Disorder 6, 24, 78
MAOI. *See* Monoamine Oxidase Inhibitor
Marital/Family Therapies 32, 56, 57
medical disorder 23, 25
medical treatments 65, 71
medication 31, 60, 65-67, 70-78
    Alprazolam 73, 76
    Amitriptyline 72, 75, 78
    Anti-adrenergic Agents 71-72, 75, 77
    Antianxiety Agents 71, 73, 76
    Anticonvulsants 73, 76, 78
    Antipsychotics 73, 76-78
    Carbamazepine 73, 76, 78
    Clonazepam 73, 76
    Clonidine 72, 75-78
    Clozapine 73, 76-78
    Desipramine 70-72, 75, 78
    Fluoxetine 70-74, 77
    Fluvoxamine 72-74, 77
    Imipramine 72-75, 78
    MAOI - Monoamine Oxidase Inhibitor 70-75, 77-78
    Nefazadone 72, 74
    Other Serotonergic Antidepressants 72, 74
    Paroxetine 70-74, 77

    Phenelzine 70-72, 74, 78
    Propranolol 72, 75-78
    Risperidone 73, 77
    Sertraline 71-72, 74, 78
    SSRI - Selective Serotonin Reuptake Inhibitor 67, 70-
        75, 77-78
    TCA - Tricyclic Antidepressant 70-73, 75, 77-78
    Thioridazine 73, 76-78
    Trazadone 72, 74
    Valproate 73, 76, 78
    What is a good strategy for PTSD pharmacotherapy? 77-78
Millon Clinical Multiaxial Inventory (MCMI) 22, 92
Minnesota Multiphasic Personality Inventory (MMPI) 22,-
    23, 84, 92
Mississippi Scale for Combat-Related PTSD (M-PTSD)
    23, 85
Monoamine Oxidase Inhibitor (MAOI) 70-75, 77-78
    Phenelzine 70-72
My Exposure to Violence (My-ETV) 23, 88
My Worst Experience Survey (MWES) 23, 87
My Worst School Experience Survey (MWSES) 23, 87

N

Nefazadone 72, 74
neurotransmitters 66, 70, 92
neutrality vs. advocacy 35, 92
nightmare 14
numbing 7-9, 12-13, 15-17, 21, 24, 28, 36, 41-43, 53, 55-
    56, 71, 73-78, 86

P

Panic Disorder 9, 24-25, 30, 69, 72-73, 77, 92
Paroxetine 72-74, 77
Peer Counseling 30, 39, 43-44
Penn Inventory 23, 85
peritraumatic dissociation 21, 92
Peritraumatic Dissociative Experiences Questionnaire 86
persistence 7
Phenelzine 72, 74, 78
physiological reactivity 12, 15
PK-Scale of the MMPI-2 23, 84
Potential Stressor Experiences Inventory (PSEI) 23, 80
Propranolol 72, 75-78
PS-Scale of the MMPI-2 23, 84
PSEI. *See* Potential Stressor Experiences Inventory
psychic numbing 9, 16, 93
psychobiological abnormalities 32, 65, 68
    Adrenergic System 68
    Corticotropin Releasing Factor (CRF) 70
    HPA System 69
    Neurotransmission 66, 70
    Serotonergic System 69
Psychodynamic Psychotherapy 44, 53, 93
psychoeducation 39, 41-43, 59, 61, 63
psychogenic amnesia 8-9, 16, 93
Psychological Debriefing 36, 39-41, 62, 93
psychological distress 3, 8, 11-12, 15

psychometric instruments 19, 22, 93
   Millon Clinical Multiaxial Inventory (MCMI) 22, 92
   Minnesota Multiphasic Personality Inventory (MMPI) 22-23, 84, 92
   Rorschach Ink Blot Test 22, 93
   Wechsler Adult Intelligence Scale (WAIS) 22, 94
psychotic disorder 77, 93
PTSD Checklist (PCL) 23, 84
PTSD Symptom Scale (PSS) 23, 84
PTSD Symptom Severity Scales 84, 89

R

recovered memories 31, 33-34
recovery 1, 4, 21, 42, 49, 58, 62
reexperiencing 3-4, 7-9, 13-15, 28, 30, 42, 73-77, 83
relapse 4-5, 30, 60, 75
remission 5
Retrospective Assessment of Traumatic Experiences 23, 81
risk factors 7, 19, 20-21
Risperidone 73, 77
Rorschach Ink Blot Test 22, 93

S

SCID. *See* Structured Clinical Interview for DSM-IV
SCL-PTSD 23, 85
secondary traumatization 56
Selective Serotonin Reuptake Inhibitor (SSRI) 67, 70-75, 77-78
   Fluoxetine 72-74, 77
   Fluvoxamine 72, 77
   Paroxetine 72, 74, 77
   Sertraline 71-72, 74, 78
self-care 35
self-report instruments 19-20, 79-80, 86-87
serotonergic system 69
Sertraline 71-72, 74, 78
severity 4, 7, 20-23, 30, 39, 52, 59-60, 75, 79-90
Sexual Experiences Survey (SES) 23, 81
Simple Phobia 24
SIT. *See* Stress Inoculation Training
Social Phobia 24
Social Rehabilitative Therapy 59-60
SSRI. *See* Selective Serotonin Reuptake Inhibitor
startle response 8, 13, 17, 24, 26
Stress Inoculation Training (SIT) 45, 49-52, 59, 61-62
Structured Clinical Interview for DSM-IV (SCID) 23, 82
Supportive Therapy 38, 56
sympathetic nervous system 66, 94
Symptom Checklist- PTSD (SCL-PTSD) 23, 85
symptom severity scales 21, 86, 89
systematic desensitization 46, 49-50, 52, 54-55

T

TCA. *See also* Tricyclic Antidepressants 70-73, 75, 77-78
The Davidson Self-Rating PTSD Scale 23, 83

Thioridazine 73, 76-78
trauma 1-5, 8-9, 12, 15-23, 25, 28-29, 31-35, 37-41, 44-48, 50, 53-57, 59, 61, 63, 67-68, 76, 79-90
trauma exposure scales 20, 79, 87
trauma focus therapy 32, 38-39, 94
trauma history 19, 29
Trauma Symptom Checklist–40 (TSC-40) 23, 85
Trauma Symptom Checklist for Children (TSCC) 23, 90
Trauma Symptom Inventory (TSI) 23, 85
traumatic event 1-3, 5, 7, 9-10, 12-14, 17-23, 33, 36, 40-43, 45-49, 53, 69, 79, 81, 86-87, 90
Traumatic Event Screening Instrument (TESI) 23, 87
Traumatic Events Questionnaire (TEQ) 23, 80
Traumatic Stress Criterion 10
Traumatic Stress Schedule (TSS) 23, 79
Trazadone 72, 74
treatments
   Assertiveness Training 46, 50-52, 59
   art & play therapy 62
   Biofeedback & Relaxation Training 46, 49, 52
   children & adolescents 27, 33-35, 44, 61-62, 87-90
   Cognitive & Behavioral Therapy 44-45, 49-52, 55-59, 61-663, 78
   Cognitive Processing Therapy 45, 48-50, 52, 55, 59
   Cognitive Therapy 45-48, 51-523, 54-56, 58, 63
   Exposure Therapy 45-48, 51-52
   Eye Movement Desensitization Reprocessing Therapy 44, 54-56
   Group Therapies 33, 57-59
   Marital/Family Therapies 32, 56, 57
   medication treatment 31, 60, 65-67, 70-78
   Peer Counseling 30, 39, 43-44
   Psychodynamic Psychotherapy 44, 53-54
   Psychoeducation 39, 41-43, 59, 61, 63
   Pscyological Debriefing 36, 39-41, 62, 93
   Stress Innocualation Training 45, 49-52, 59, 61-62
   Trauma Focus Therapy 32, 38-39, 94
Tricyclic Antidepressants (TCAs). *See also* TCA 70-75, 77-78
   Amitriptyline 72, 75, 78
   Desipramine 72, 75, 78
   Imipramine 72, 75, 78

V

Valproate 73, 76, 78
vicarious traumatization 35-37, 58, 94

W

Wechsler Adult Intelligence Scale (WAIS) 22, 94
When Bad Things Happen Scale (WBTHS) 23, 87
Women's Wartime Stressor Scale (WWSS) 23, 82
Wyatt Sex History Questionnaire (WSHQ) 23, 81

Comments about the book: _____
                              Name of Book

_____

_____

_____

_____

Other titles you want Compact Clinicals to offer:

_____

_____

_____

_____

Please provide your name and address in the space below to be placed on our mailing list.

_____

_____

_____

_____

Compact Clinicals

Ordering in three easy steps:

1 **Please fill out completely:**

Billing/Shipping Information

Individual/Company _____ Department/Mail Stop _____

Profession _____

Street Address/P.O. Box _____

City, State, Zip _____

Telephone _____ ☐ Ship to residence ☐ Ship to business

2 **Here's what I'd like to order:**

Book Name	Book Qty.	Unit Price	Total
Attention Deficit Hyperactivity Disorder (in Adults and Children) The Latest Assessment and Treatment Strategies		$14.95	
Borderline Personality Disorder The Latest Assessment and Treatment Strategies		$14.95	
Conduct Disorders The Latest Assessment and Treatment Strategies		$14.95	
Major Depressive Disorder The Latest Assessment and Treatment Strategies		$14.95	
Obsessive Compulsive Disorder The Latest Assessment and Treatment Strategies		$14.95	
Post-Traumatic Stress Disorder The Latest Assessment and Treatment Strategies		$14.95	

Subtotal _____

Tax Add (6.725% in MO) _____

Shipping Fee
Add ($3.75 for the first book and $1.00 for each additional book) _____

Total Amount _____

3 **Payment Method:** Telephone Orders/Toll Free: 1(800)408-8830 • Fax Orders to: 1(816)587-7198
Send Postal Orders to: Compact Clinicals • 7205 NW Waukomis Dr., Suite A • Kansas City, MO 64151

☐ Check Enclosed
☐ Please charge to my:

○ Visa   Name on Card _____

○ MasterCard   Cardholder Signature _____

○ Discover Card Account #/Exp. Date _ _ _ _ - _ _ _ _ - _ _ _ _ - _ _ _ _ (_ _/_ _)

Comments about the book: _____

Name of Book

_____   _____

_____

_____

_____

Other titles you want Compact Clinicals to offer:

_____   _____

_____

_____

_____

Please provide your name and address in the space below to be placed on our mailing list.

_____

_____

_____

_____

Compact Clinicals

Ordering in three easy steps:

1 **Please fill out completely:**

Billing/Shipping Information

Individual/Company _____ Department/Mail Stop _____

Profession _____

Street Address/P.O. Box _____

City, State, Zip _____

Telephone _____ ☐ Ship to residence ☐ Ship to business

2 **Here's what I'd like to order:**

Book Name	Book Qty.	Unit Price	Total
Attention Deficit Hyperactivity Disorder (in Adults and Children) The Latest Assessment and Treatment Strategies		$14.95	
Borderline Personality Disorder The Latest Assessment and Treatment Strategies		$14.95	
Conduct Disorders The Latest Assessment and Treatment Strategies		$14.95	
Major Depressive Disorder The Latest Assessment and Treatment Strategies		$14.95	
Obsessive Compulsive Disorder The Latest Assessment and Treatment Strategies		$14.95	
Post-Traumatic Stress Disorder The Latest Assessment and Treatment Strategies		$14.95	

Subtotal ☐

Tax Add (6.725% in MO) ☐

Shipping Fee ☐
Add ($3.75 for the first book and $1.00 for each additional book)

Total Amount ☐

3 **Payment Method:** Telephone Orders/Toll Free: 1(800)408-8830 • Fax Orders to: 1(816)587-7198
Send Postal Orders to: Compact Clinicals • 7205 NW Waukomis Dr., Suite A • Kansas City, MO 64151
☐ Check Enclosed
☐ Please charge to my:
  ◯ Visa   Name on Card _____
  ◯ MasterCard   Cardholder Signature _____
  ◯ Discover Card Account #/Exp. Date _ _ _ _ - _ _ _ _ - _ _ _ _ - _ _ _ _ (_ _/_ _)

© Compact Clinicals